Super Soul Food
with Cousin Rosie

Super Soul Food

with
Cousin Rosie

100+ MODERN TWISTS ON COMFORT FOOD CLASSICS

ROSIE MAYES

Photography and styling by
Michael and Danielle Kartes

SASQUATCH BOOKS
SEATTLE

This book is dedicated to my awesome son, Giovanni, and my amazing husband, Anthony. I'd also like to dedicate this book to my online cousins!

CONTENTS

Foreword 1 / Introduction 3 / The Super Soul Food Pantry 9

RISE AND GRIND 29

WANNA BE STARTIN' SOMETHIN' 53

BREAKIN' BREAD 85

THE HALVES AND HAVE HOTS 107

MAIN SQUEEZES 123

SIDE PIECES 163

SOMETHIN' SWEET 185

SIPPIN' TIPSY 223

Acknowledgments 237 / Index 239

RECIPE LIST

RISE AND GRIND

Red Velvet Waffles 30
Cinnamon Toast Crunch French Toast 33
Southern Fried Cinnamon Apples 34
Ultimate Breakfast Sandwich 35
Egg, Sausage, and Potato Scramble 36
Soulful Breakfast Enchiladas 39
Steak and Cheese Omelette 41
Meat Lover's Quiche 42
Waffle Fried Chicken 45
Five-Cheese Hash Brown Casserole 47
Stuffed Hash Browns 48
Cheddar, Ham, and Grits Casserole 51

WANNA BE STARTIN' SOMETHIN'

Turnip Greens and Artichoke Au Gratin
   Dip 55
Voodoo Dip 56
Cajun Blooming Onions 59
Creole Loaded Potato Skins 61
Bacon-Wrapped Stuffed Jalapeños 65
Loaded Baked Oysters 66
Grilled Creole Shrimp Cocktails 67
Fried Salmon Bites 71
Creole Crab Cakes with Sweet Chili
   Sauce 72
Poached Garlic Crab Legs 74
Royal Wings 75
Fried Chicken Gizzards 76

Fried Chicken Sliders 79
Boudin Balls 80
Southern Meat Pies with Creole
   Chimichurri 82

BREAKIN' BREAD

Hot-Water Cornbread 86
Cracklin' Cornbread 88
Savory Monkey Bread 91
Three-Cheese, Bacon, and Herb
   Biscuits 92
Garlicky Cheese Drop Biscuits 94
Red Velvet Biscuits 95
Cherry Pie Biscuits 96
Butter Pecan Scones 99
Hummingbird Bread 100
Apple Fritter Bread 101
Real Deal Beignets 104

THE HALVES AND HAVE HOTS

Not Yo' Mama's Bacon Caesar Salad 108
Cousin Rosie's Macaroni Salad 110
Mardi Gras Pasta Salad 111
Cajun Chicken Pasta Salad 113
Fried Tilapia Sandwiches 114
Muffuletta 117
Spicy Catfish and Oyster Po'boys 118
Country Steak Chili 120

MAIN SQUEEZES

Jamaican Jerk Shrimp and Peppers 124
Blackened Salmon 127
Seafood Lasagna 128
Seafood Boil with Creole Garlic Sauce 131
Butterflied Herb-Roasted Chicken 133
Bacon-Wrapped Stuffed Chicken
    Thighs 134
Best Damn Chicken and Dumplings 136
Easy Smoked Whole Turkey 139
Slow Cooker Smothered Turkey Wings 141
Deep-Fried Cornish Game Hens 145
Philly Cheesesteak Lasagna 147
Easy Slow Cooker Short Ribs 151
Jamaican Oxtails 152
Grilled Lamb Chops 155
Cajun-Style Leg of Lamb 156
Stuffed Pork Chops 157
Blackberry-Glazed Ribs 158
Slow Cooker Neck Bones and
    Potatoes 161

SIDE PIECES

Soulful Cabbage and Collard Greens 164
Creamed Spinach with Bacon 166
Southern Broccoli Casserole 167
Collard Green and Smoked Turkey
    Dressing 168
Creamy Mashed Baby Reds 170
Roasted Parsnips with Bacon 172
Creole Street Corn 173
Fresh Creamed Corn 175
Corn Pudding Casserole 176
Pigeon Peas and Rice 177
White Beans and Sausage 179

Orzo Rice Pilaf 180
Southern Baked Macaroni and Cheese
    Casserole 182

SOMETHIN' SWEET

Southern Tea Cakes 186
Better-Than-Sex Cookies 188
Rolo Brownies 191
Salted Caramel and Chocolate Chip
    Cookies 192
King Cake 193
Peach Cobbler Bread Pudding 197
Cherries and Cream Funnel Cakes 198
Blackberry Pie 199
Chocolate Chess Pie 203
Chocolate Cornbread Cheesecake 204
Strawberry Shortcake Cheesecake 207
Caramel Cake 210
Coconut Cake 213
Moist 7UP Cake 215
The Ultimate Carrot Cake 218
Three-Layer Key Lime Cake with Key Lime
    Buttercream Frosting 220

SIPPIN' TIPSY

Easy Strawberry Lemonade 224
Pink Moscato Lemonade 227
Pineapple Hennyrita 228
Frozen Green Sweet Tea 229
Grown Folks Peach Sweet Tea 230
Boss Lady Cocktail 232
Cherry Mojito 233
Island Girl Cocktail 234

FOREWORD

Have you ever been to a good friend's house and from the time you walked through their door, slipped off your shoes, and sat on their couch, you were at ease? The food's on, the drink's on its way to you, and you can just relax and be yourself. It's a rare treat to find a friend like this. The only thing that's required of you is that you be truly yourself. This is the Rosie Mayes I've come to know over the last several years. Rosie is a woman who makes you feel like you can truly just be who you are, no questions asked. She is strong, determined, and wise. She has a light touch in her cooking and an old soul.

I first met Rosie three years ago, but I immediately felt like I'd known her for years. I had recently begun cooking through and styling her first book, *I Heart Soul Food*, and I knew immediately that she was special. We met at a Seattle studio, the plan being to photograph a few of the dishes in the book and to make some portraits of Rosie. When she threw on a little Cardi B during the cover shoot, I knew Rosie was the real one. From that point on, Rosie has become more than a client. She's the friend you've always wanted to have in your corner.

Soul food asks you to share. Soul food asks you to give. And soul food asks you to love in a way you might not have before. It's a style of cooking that is abundant and spicy and loaded with flavor. Rosie gave me a look at a way of cooking and of living that keeps me coming back for more. Her fun and straightforward point of view in the kitchen is exactly what every home cook needs.

Rosie's imprint in the food and cooking world is electric and authentic. She is asking no one's permission and living her life out in a way that is so dang inspiring. With this follow-up book, *Super Soul Food with Cousin Rosie*, I can't even begin to tell you how brilliant the food truly is. It's got the right amount of kick and love and heat! It's got soul, style, and a life all its own that is an extension of the Rosie we know and love.

Get into your kitchen, get with your people, and don't stop cooking. You will be a better cook for learning from her—prepare to level up! Soul food Rosie-style has a way of doing that. This woman is the real deal, one of a kind. Enjoy!

—Danielle Kartes

INTRODUCTION

Welcome to my house, where everyone is invited and we do big, bold, soul food flavors that might surprise you . . . with that little something extra you've come to know, love, and crave from your Cousin Rosie. In this, my second book, I'm building on my Cajun and Creole Louisiana roots and combining them with my Pacific Northwest love for seafood and fresh flavors. On my blog (IHeartRecipes.com), my YouTube channel (I Heart Recipes), and in my first book (*I Heart Soul Food*), I brought my Southern roots into my Seattle kitchen and shared with the world everything my mom taught me, everything my grandmother taught her, and all my inherited, long-nurtured love of soul food.

The recipes in this book represent a time in my life when I am growing and changing, and I'm going to share that journey with you. Here you'll find brand-new *and* fan-favorite recipes, all of them classic soul food with a little Cousin Rosie twist. My first book contained all the traditional dishes of my youth and classic recipes we know and love, and in this book, I've taken the soul food I love so much and made it sing—the dishes are brighter, bolder, saucier, and the volume has been turned way up! You'll be asking yourself why you never made a Philly cheesesteak lasagna before! And you'll certainly be adding my grandmother Rosa Mae's waffle fried chicken to your lineup.

My love of soul food started early. I was just three or four when my aunt Frances first brought me into the kitchen and let me cook alongside her. I just did what she did, playing and learning at the same time. Eating that food, then beginning to make it, set up a lifelong respect for preparing dishes that both feed the body and warm the heart. By the time I was five, I had stepped up to the stove to make real food by myself, cooking up a big ol' batch of my favorite spaghetti, which became my signature dish. Everyone in the family makes something they're known for. These are dishes that the family looks forward to! To this day, I make my spaghetti just the same way I did at five. It's a winner.

My mother was a hardworking single mom. She'd bring me along with her, my grandmother, and my aunties to the Parkside Nursing Home in Seattle, where they whipped up giant batches of macaroni and cheese, meatloaf, and gumbo for the residents. My mother, grandmother, and aunties were *in charge* in that kitchen, and this inspired me. I would choose to be nowhere else than in that kitchen with those great ladies showing me the way.

As I grew, it became my job to get dinner fixed while my mom was working. At first, I'd follow her recipes to a T, no adding or taking away. But as I became a better cook, I started to experiment a little here and there. My mom would tell me, "No playin' in the kitchen!" She'd tell me how the older generation didn't want anything messed with in their classic dishes. "Leave those recipes alone and stick to the plan!" But I just couldn't help myself! I started adding more spices, more flavor. I love my mom, she is incredible, but I can still hear her saying: "Cornbread is *not sweet!*" But there I went, making it all kinds of ME! (My sweet cornbread is incredible, I might add.) I'd add cheese, fresh corn, or herbs to come up with something not only delicious but *different* from the dishes we ate in our community. I'd dig into the freezer or pantry to see exactly what we had on hand, and I'd use it to make food that no one could touch, flavor-wise. That was the beginning of my personal style, my culinary journey. I'd taken my food education from my family, then began mixing it with who I was as a cook and a woman.

Fast forward to my husband, Anthony. I wanted to cook him food he loved and integrate my style, and let me tell you: that man is always happy when I fix him anything! When we had our son, Giovanni, I knew I wanted him to cook like I had when I was younger. When he was just three years old, he saw a man cooking on TV, and that really helped him. I can remember him saying "Mom, he looks like *me!*" He is now a teenager and *so good* in the kitchen, and that makes me proud. When he wants to make something his own, I am all for it.

Where we come from plays such an important role in our cooking styles. My grandma Rosa Mae—my mom's mom, my namesake, and after whom I've named my seasonings company (RosaMae Seasonings)—was a strong woman who accomplished what she set her mind to. I have a natural entrepreneurial spirit that I know has been in my line for generations. I inherited tenacity from her. I learned to be all about my business and work hard. Flavoring my food has always been a cornerstone in my cooking, so the seasoning line was a natural step for me. We each have an opportunity and obligation to leave a legacy for our children, and I want my son to know he can do anything he sets his mind to.

My grandmother did this for me simply by living her life. She—and her husband, my grandfather—left Baton Rouge during the Great Migration and headed north for a better life, pregnant with the first of what would be eighteen children—six girls, twelve boys. I had so many aunts who made sure I knew how to cook! They landed in Seattle, and as the family grew, my grandmother became the queen bee of an always-busy kitchen. She was a real Southern belle, constantly whipping up Creole and Cajun dishes to feed her

family (and some of the neighbors too). Eventually all those children began having kids of their own, and that's why I'm known as Cousin Rosie. Though my relatives are now firmly rooted in the Pacific Northwest, all that soul food helped us remember our Southern roots and where we came from.

With a giant family like that, every gathering was an event, but one day of the year always took even our big appetites beyond their wildest dreams: Christmas! It was the biggest, most delicious celebration you've ever seen. We would have a turkey, a ham, *and* a giant pot of gumbo on the table. There were collard greens, candied yams, and my mom's famous potato salad. But the best part was all the desserts. My grandparents didn't have enough money to afford gifts for all the children, so their present was the Christmas dessert table. You could always find me, little Rosie, stealing a pinch from the sweets before we served up any of the cakes or puddings or pies. Tradition has this way of bringing back the good things about the past and opening our hearts to welcome the future. I know that I wouldn't have had it any other way. Tables full of dishes that bring back and honor those lean times are what I'm all about—I am going to find a way to make something out of nothing and move on. Keep those gifts and pass me the red velvet cheese-cake! Set another place at the table for the fresh cousins coming up and give me all the laughter. So many of the recipes in these pages are perfect for family gatherings and holidays so you can do the same.

My beloved grandma passed when I was only two, but I carry on her legacy as a cook in my kitchen and in my name: she was Rosa Mae, and I was named Rosemary after her. Funny, the name Mayes comes from my husband! My grandfather cared for me and brought me up, sharing photos of my grand-mother and telling me all the stories about her—stories revolving around the fantastic meals that came from her kitchen. I grew up eating dishes made from recipes that had been passed down to her daughters, but somehow I ended up being the only one in my generation who followed in her culinary footsteps. When my cousins need a taste of home, Cousin Rosie is the one they call.

I consider my online audience my "cousins" too—and they call on me for beloved family recipes just like my real cousins do. It is immensely rewarding to share this passion for soul food with the world. But at some point, I noticed that a lot of my friends didn't know their way around the kitchen. They weren't fortunate enough to get their grandmother's oxtail recipes from their mom or to learn to fry pork chops with their aunt Frances. So I became the friend that everyone could go to for help in the kitchen. Eventually it grew beyond a hobby, and my husband suggested I do something more with it.

And he was right. I was burnt out working twelve-hour days as a certified nursing assistant in end-of-life care, and my life needed a shake-up.

One day, I posted a video of myself making dinner—fried chicken, macaroni and cheese, and peas—and the internet went nuts. There weren't a lot of soul food blogs out there—it was almost like soul food didn't exist online—but people were hungry for a taste of home. They wanted to know how to make the food their grandmothers made. There were all sorts of niches that were filled by other blogs, but not this one. I knew that there had to be an audience for authentic soul food, and that first video proved it.

From there, I created my blog and YouTube channel and focused on Southern and soul food. For a while, I was juggling them with my full-time job. But then big companies saw what I was doing and recognized that what I had created was a worthwhile investment. And I was ready to jump in with both feet! I've gained a lot of online family members via YouTube, my blog, Facebook, Pinterest, and even Instagram. That's why I'm always Cousin Rosie—online and in person.

When it came time to write this next book, it came naturally. My cookbooks are really an extension of who I am at the time and who I have always been. Folks visiting my blog and Facebook page really nudged me to get into the book-writing world, and I am so glad I did! It feels like such a gift that my roots and traditions are now a part of feeding other people's families and hearts. It was the obvious choice to do another book with my takes on the classics—not your mama's soul food, but Cousin Rosie's twists through and through. My fans know what they like, and that always includes me remixing the standbys. Like Creole loaded potato skins, or steak and cheese omelettes, or smothered turkey wings, or Jamaican oxtails . . . who's getting hungry? I know I am!

Over the last few years in this cooking game, I've learned that I love seasonings and spices, quality ingredients and freshness. You will see fresh herb and seasoning blends in this book, and you are going to see spices used in unexpected ways. Say goodbye to simply using salt for a flavor boost! You are going to cry happy tears after trying my blackberry-glazed ribs! Yes, I said *blackberry* and *ribs*, and I can't wait for you to get to it! I want you to make these dishes for your family and to use them as inspiration to do your own thing in the kitchen. Spice up that same ol' recipe, use the cuts of meat you like, and see what happens. Spoiler alert: I've seen how it goes—it's pretty good. You've got a friend and cousin in me, so get in the kitchen and start feeding the people you love.

THE SUPER SOUL FOOD PANTRY

When you want the food you crave, it's not a matter of getting a restaurant to fix it for you. By planning right and stocking your fridge and pantry, you'd be surprised what you can whip up at home. Even spending a little extra on quality ingredients or splurges at the grocery store will still cost you far less than ordering that same food at a restaurant. For example, if you never like to buy rib eyes at the store because they cost $14.99 a pound, think of it this way: when you go out to eat, you are looking at $50 to $60 for that one-pound steak. I'm going to share with you what I keep on hand to make great food at home. Nothing wrong with going out, but in my opinion, it's better when its homemade.

Readers of my first book will recognize most of the staples mentioned in this chapter—that's because they are my tried-and-trues. If these are familiar ingredients and tools that you already have around, go ahead and flip to the recipes to get cooking!

I like to cook with what I have on hand—to make something out of nothing—so every time I consider what to make, the first step is to open the pantry. If you are always buying things that support your pantry, you will save money *and* create delicious food with ease.

The key to cooking like this is to have a well-stocked pantry, and that includes the freezer! Mine tends to be overflowing, because when I grocery shop, I try to get things that get my imagination going. Whatever pops into my head, that's what I put in the cart—especially in my favorite aisles: the seafood and baking sections.

This style works for me because I've got a super soul food pantry on hand, with shelf after shelf of all my favorite ingredients. Seasonings and spices have a long pull date, so you can stock up and draw from them, only replenishing from season to season; the same goes for dry goods. Let this chapter serve as a guide to get your own pantry going. Fill it with things you love. And take a page from my book, literally, and use my suggestions for easy dinner prep.

I suggest a few of my favorite brands for some products, but don't feel like you must get these exact ones—soul food is all about making do with what you can easily find and what you can afford. Love is the most important ingredient, but don't you skimp on the herbs and spices! I want you to draw from the things *you* love as far as pantry staples go. If your favorite type of rice is not listed in my go-tos, by all means keep doing YOU!

Super soul food—saucy, dreamy, spicy, and flavorful—comes from deep down. It begs you to consider family and your own life experiences. I know you are absolutely ready to get started. You are going to change your tastes a bit and improve on the classics. Give yourself a chance to blossom!

A LOOK IN MY PANTRY

Spice It Up

I am so passionate about seasoning that I launched my own seasoning line! RosaMae Seasonings covers everything you might ever need, but you don't need *my* seasonings to get started. Just make sure you get a variety of seasonings *you* love! We can't hide from the fact that we've got a huge hypertension problem in the Black community, so for flavor I've added a lot of herbs and spices to my super soul food in place of all the salt we may normally use. Here are my faves.

Bay leaves: Nobody can ever explain what bay leaves do, but they just sort of make everything taste better! You can't skip them in your short ribs.

Black pepper (ground, coarse, and cracked): Black pepper is an essential piece of the soul food flavor puzzle, and I use it in three different sizes of grind. If you have a pepper grinder, you can do this yourself by twisting the grinder—ground will be almost a powder, fine enough to disappear into dishes; coarse, a little bit bigger so that you can see it in salad dressings and such; and cracked pepper is even bigger, almost like peppercorn flakes, and will add texture and be visible at the end of the dish.

Cajun seasoning: The base is similar to Creole seasoning, but Cajun food begs for spice, so it's also got red pepper flakes, cayenne pepper, and white pepper. My favorite brand is called Tone's.

Creole seasoning: This is similar to seasoning salt, but with the addition of a few herbs and spices—you can make it yourself, but I just buy Tony Cachere's. Or mine! You can also grab this in a salt-free version. It works for my boudin balls (and so much more).

Garlic powder: Along with fresh garlic, the powder creates layers of flavors in many soul food dishes.

Kosher salt: All my recipes are tested with kosher salt (the standard for cooking).

Lemon pepper: I love the convenience of this mix of lemon oil, salt, and black pepper. I use it on my chicken, seafood, and pork.

The Real Deal on Seasoning

Have you ever had someone's cooking and they overseasoned?! Well, I have, and there's no way to fix that at the table. There have been times when I've eaten food so salty that I thought I was going to pass out. That's why I'm super careful when it comes to seasoning, doing my best to get it just right and never overdo it. But if you're going to season wrong, you want to underseason—if you underseason a dish, people can always add salt and pepper once it's on their plate. If you overseason, you will be talked about! Feel free to adjust seasonings to your likings, but take it easy. Especially if you're serving others.

Let's also start thinking about flavor versus salt. In our community, it's no secret we deal with hypertension and blood sugar issues. We need to not be afraid to use fresh herbs, pick up salt-free seasonings, and even add fresh lemon juice to dishes to cut back on our salt intake. This goes a long way in making soulfully delicious dishes. Just because a recipe calls for a certain amount of salt, it doesn't mean you *have* to add that much. Feel free to cut back and add flavor in other ways.

Old Bay Seasoning: This is a classic seafood seasoning. I always mix it into the cornmeal and flour for fried seafood, or directly onto shrimp or lobster.

Onion powder: The powerful, savory flavor of onion powder will punch up any boring dish.

Paprika: Few dishes are complete without the stunning dots of red that come from paprika.

Parsley flakes: I must have some color (like paprika), and the green of this dried herb lights up any dark stews or beans.

Poultry seasoning: Another McCormick favorite, this mix of thyme, sage, and other herby flavors always finds its way onto my chicken and turkey.

Red pepper flakes: I can't help it—I always want to add red pepper flakes to give a little kick to a dish.

Seasoning salt: I make my own version, mixing kosher salt, garlic powder, onion powder, black pepper, and a little paprika (for color), but if you'd rather buy some, a favorite is my own RosaMae Seasonings.

Thyme: I love to use fresh thyme, but dried herbs work too—they are cheap and don't go bad, which is good because I need plenty of thyme for all of my bean dishes!

Fresh herbs are my go-to these days to add a bit of green natural flavor and color. There are generally two families of herbs I turn to: woody herbs and tender herbs. Woody herbs have a wood-like stem (rosemary, sage, and thyme, for example), and tender herbs have an edible stem (like chives, parsley, and cilantro). Here are some favorites of mine to keep on hand.

Cilantro: Are you team soap or team herby deliciousness? This tender herb divides the group right down the middle. It's great in dishes with heat or creaminess, and it's traditional in Mexican cuisine. Cilantro isn't traditional soul food fare, but this is Rosie's cookin' with a twist, so it goes just fine.

Italian/flat-leaf parsley: I use dried parsley in so many dishes, but lately I've been loving finishing a dish with a sprinkle of finely chopped fresh parsley. This herb is a bit bitter, bright, and has a very green flavor. It even has that spicy undertone you'd expect from a mustard green, only milder without any heat. Parsley adds depth to soups, stews, and slow cooker recipes.

Marjoram: This big-flavored woody herb is great in Creole cooking. For me it's very similar to rosemary and thyme: earthy and delicious. It has some bitterness and subtle citrus notes.

Oregano: Fresh oregano is floral and earthy and just right for anything Italian. This woody herb holds up nicely to beef, lamb, and chicken. You'll find it in so many spice blends for Creole cooking. Fresh oregano adds some kick without the heat when you need it.

Rosemary: This herb looks like tiny pine tree clippings and smells like heaven. Toss some into that lamb chop marinade!

Thyme: You'll find this in all jerk recipes, and it makes its way into every holiday classic. It's a staple in poultry seasoning and marries well with oxtail. This guy is easy to grow, so get planting!

Bake It Better

My saucy, soulful kitchen always has everything you can think of for baking on hand. I like to make sure I have multiple kinds of flour and sugar and fat. You'll need dark brown sugar and regular white sugar for some recipes. Good cocoa powder and a few kinds of oil. I love shortening for flakiness and real butter for flavor. When I hit the grocery store, I like to stock up on things like canned pineapple and evaporated milk, because you never know when you might wanna whip up, say, my hummingbird cake. This isn't everything in my baking pantry, but it's a great start if you are just building one.

All-purpose flour: As the name implies, this flour does everything—baking, frying, and even thickening gravies. I prefer the Pillsbury version.

Baking soda and baking powder: These are leavening agents, so you'll need them to make sure your baked goods rise. Any brand will work, as long as the package isn't too old—they lose their potency over time.

Brown sugar: I use brown sugar (either dark or light) in most of my desserts, but I'll also sneak it into red sauces to bring down the acidity.

Cake flour: Finer than all-purpose flour, cake flour makes my cakes lighter and fluffier. Before I really got into baking, my grandmother-in-law tipped me off that Swans Down is the best, so that's what I try to have on hand.

Canned fruits and pie fillings: You'll almost always find me cooking down my own fresh fruit and sugar, but that doesn't mean we can't enjoy a shortcut, so I like to have a bit of crushed pineapple or apple pie filling on hand for a quick cheat in a recipe. I love to have canned pie fillings just hanging out for a rainy day.

Canned milk: Evaporated milk is a must in my kitchen pantry. The milk is cooked down to remove the excess water, and it is shelf stable and can last years if you need. Evaporated milk will never curdle, so it's great for adding richness to pies or cakes or breads. It's affordable and really calls on our grandmothers' preferences, because there isn't a granny I know who isn't using canned milk to add oomph to her pies.

Cornmeal: I use Albers yellow cornmeal, which is finely ground, because that's what my mom and her mom before her used, so I know it makes my cornbread and seafood breading just how I like it.

Cornstarch: Buy whatever brand is on sale, but you will want to have this around to thicken gravies and dessert fillings.

Gluten-free flour: If you eat gluten-free, chances are you already know what flours you like to cook with. If you are new to gluten-free cooking though, I really like Bob's Red Mill 1-to-1 Baking Flour. It's basically a cup-for-cup flour replacement blend. If one of my recipes calls for 1 cup all-purpose or self-rising flour, feel free to use 1 cup gluten-free baking flour as a substitute. You can also follow the instructions on page 16 to make your own gluten-free self-rising flour.

Granulated sugar: This is just regular white sugar—everything needs a little a sweetness. I usually buy C&H brand for all my sugars.

Nonstick baking spray: Baker's Joy makes sliding your baked goods out of the pan so much easier—it's a mix of oil and flour without the mess of greasing a pan and then dusting it.

Nonstick cooking spray: Spray cans make greasing things way easier—it's just oil, but less fuss. I use PAM.

Powdered sugar: You need this on hand for baking to create icings and frostings for all those fabulous desserts—and to top your beignets and biscuits!

Self-rising flour: I reach for this premade mix (it has baking soda and rising agents) when making biscuits, but I also love it for any kind of frying because it helps make stuff come out extra crispy. If you can't find it, you can make your own with 1 cup all-purpose flour (or gluten-free flour blend) plus 1½ teaspoons baking powder and ¼ teaspoon fine kosher salt.

Sugar substitutes: Listen, it's not lost on me that we all want to cut back on our sugar these days. But we don't have to rely on sugar and salt for all our flavor. There are some excellent sugar substitutes on the market, and there is no shame in lightening up whatever dish you need to for your tastes and dietary needs.

Vanilla extract: This is a baking essential, but it can be a bit expensive, so I like to buy the Kirkland Signature brand at Costco or whatever is on sale. It's just important to make sure that it's pure vanilla, not imitation, because it does taste different.

Fatten Up That Fridge

Butter (salted and unsalted): My grandmother always used Darigold butter, a local company here in the Northwest, so it's what I purchase. I generally use salted butter, but if you don't like it as much, use unsalted and add salt to taste.

Buttermilk: I love using buttermilk in desserts. If you can't find it, make it yourself by stirring a tablespoon of lemon juice or distilled white vinegar into a cup of milk and letting it stand for ten minutes.

Cheese: My favorite cheeses are sharp cheddar and Havarti—you'll see them over and over in my recipes, along with a few others. I mostly pick up the Boar's Head brand.

Eggs: I usually buy large eggs. The store brand is fine: I go through a lot, and I need them to be affordable.

Half-and-half: This is just a mix of heavy cream and milk, so if you don't have it on hand, just mix them one-to-one.

Heavy cream: This is an essential for baking and making frosting.

Milk: I always use whole milk in my recipes; there's no low-fat stuff here. But again, if you need to lighten something up for your needs, your girl is right behind you saying that's okay!

Savory Essentials

Bell peppers: I like really dark-green or red bell peppers.

Broth and stock: I simply do not have the time to be making all the broths and stocks that I use in my kitchen. I buy vegetable broth (for greens dishes), beef broth (for oxtails and roasts), and chicken broth (for most everything else).

Canned tomatoes: For spaghetti, I'll need tomatoes to make that red sauce. But I also add them to stews, and my Louisiana family members say I'm weird, but I like them in my gumbo.

Dried beans: I've always got pinto beans to cook up with ham hocks, and red beans to cook with stronger flavors like sausage and smoked turkey.

Sorting Beans 101

Dried beans are my go-to. They are affordable and delicious, and they pack a large amount of protein. When times are lean, you can pretty much rely on dried beans to get you through. Many people don't know how to properly care for them though. Here's what to do:

1   Get a white plate and pour out a layer of beans. The white plate helps you see things that shouldn't be there. You'd be surprised, but you are looking for rocks, sticks, and bits of debris.
2   Pick out any broken or discolored beans and get rid of them.
3   Rinse the beans. Put them in a colander if they are big enough, or use a mesh strainer if they are smaller beans or lentils. Rinse them well in cool water. I usually rinse mine twice.

Once you finish, soak and cook the beans! There are so many methods for bringing dried beans back to creamy goodness. For a fast soak, simply bring a pot of beans covered with 2 to 3 inches of water *above* the beans to a rolling boil for 2 minutes, then turn the heat off and let them soak for at least 1 hour. The longer you let them sit, the faster they will cook in your stew. For a slower soak, a very popular method is to let them sit in cool water overnight. This allows them to get tender enough for cooking while you sleep.

Trust me, if you throw dry beans into a pot without prepping them first, you won't get a creamy textured bean. It'll be crumbly and not good. Take the extra time to sort and soak 'em right.

Garlic: I love garlic. I usually have fresh garlic on hand, but I always have preminced garlic as well.

Green onions: The fattest stems and the brightest colors bring that soft onion flavor that can't be beat! Finish off appetizers and mains with it; it gives that bit of green you might be craving, along with a little crunch.

Hot sauce: Listen, I love hot sauce. I use many different kinds, and you will find hot sauce everywhere in the super soul food kitchen! So my advice is: try them all. You'll settle on one or five that are a must for you.

Ketchup: It's a condiment, but you want to keep enough around to cook with too. Either way, I stick to the standard Heinz.

Leafy greens: Don't think that greens just means collards. Swiss chard, rainbow chard, spinach, mustard greens, turnip greens, beet greens—you can eat all of them!

Mayonnaise: Everybody has a favorite mayonnaise based on what they grew up with. For me, that's Hellmann's/Best Foods. If you have a different favorite, that's okay—use that.

Mustard: When I say mustard, I'm talking about the throwback, classic standard yellow stuff from French's, nothing fancy. However, I do use Dijon mustard when it comes to my Blooming Onion.

Olive oil: Olive is the best oil for sautéing vegetables and dressing salads, and I especially like the kind from the Oilerie, which can be found online.

Pasta: I make a lot of macaroni and cheese and spaghetti, so I always have elbows and spaghetti noodles on hand. I never know if someone's going to stop by, and I can whip those up in a second.

Potatoes: Russet potatoes are cheap and work in nearly all my potato dishes. I stick to the medium size because they're easy to peel and cut.

Vegetable oil: I mostly use Mazola corn oil because it's what my mom and aunts use, especially for deep-frying, but I switch to canola for baking.

White rice: Rice is mostly a filler in my kitchen, so the type is not super important, but it should be long grain.

Worcestershire sauce: This is a key ingredient to add a little saltiness and flavor to dishes.

Yellow and red onions: I use yellow onions—my favorite is our local Walla Walla variety—and big shiny red onions. I look for ones where the papery peel is a bit broken so I can see that they're not brown inside.

Prepping Greens 101

When I was a little girl, we had greens every single night with dinner. Greens weren't my favorite as a kid, but I can't get enough now.

Folks often chop the tops off their favorite veggies and throw them out—don't do that! Even radish greens are spicy and savory and will give you that heat when you sauté them or chop them up for a salad. When you render down a bit of bacon, or add smoked turkey wings or ham hocks, you are always in for a treat. I'm known for mixing cabbage with collards these days, and I always serve up a silky, smoky plate of greens next to every meal.

Let's talk cleaning! Even precleaned bagged greens need a rinse. All greens (except spinach and cabbage) need a good cleaning before you cook them, some more than others. Start by separating all the leaves and tossing them into a clean sink (I usually bleach my sink down before cleaning my greens). Once they're in the sink, rinse them well, swishing them to get off any dirt. Next, fill the sink with lukewarm water, 1 tablespoon salt, and ¼ cup apple cider vinegar. Let the greens soak for 30 minutes, then rub them using your fingertips. Drain the water and rinse the leaves. Repeat the steps until the sink is grit- and dirt-free. (If you don't want to trouble with the entire sink, you can use a large mixing bowl or a food-grade bin instead.)

Now you're ready to start chopping. For leaves with a thick stem, I fold each leaf in half so that the rib—extending from the stem all the way up the center of the leaf—runs along one edge, then I cut that out and compost it. You can easily rip the stem away from the leaf as well. For softer greens, like spinach, you don't need to bother with this step. Once any stems are removed, you can stack a few leaves at a time and chop them up into the desired size.

Get creative with your greens, and don't ever throw out turnip or beet greens again!

ALL MY TOOLS

I cook soul food, so my kitchen is pretty bare-bones. You don't need to spend a lot of money to make great food. There are a few appliances that I love because they make my life easier and my cleanup process simpler—like my beloved deep fryer—but for the most part, this is just a list of what I keep in my kitchen. I cook the way I do because I'm always looking for what's quick, affordable, and not too complicated—and most of that comes from how I cook, not what sort of tools I'm using.

9-by-13-inch baking dish: The clear Pyrex type is my go-to baking dish, but sometimes I'll bake a lasagna or something in a fancier casserole dish if I'm bringing it to a party.

Aluminum foil: Since baking dishes don't usually come with oven-safe tops, I use foil when I need to cover food in the oven.

Bundt pan: A large Bundt is what I use to make my pound cakes and 7UP Cake. If it's not nonstick, you'll want to use baking spray.

Colander: Obviously you need a colander to drain pasta, but they're also great for rinsing vegetables.

Deep fryer: One place I do have a strong opinion is the deep fryer. I use a Hamilton Beach 12-cup capacity with a basket. It heats up fast, I can drop a lot of food in at once, I don't have to fish around for pieces of food in the oil, and it's easy to clean. If you don't have a deep fryer, I recommend that you use a 12-inch cast-iron pan and a candy/deep-fry thermometer to measure your temperatures.

Dry measuring cups: Cheap steel handheld measuring cups work great and are better than plastic because the measurements are etched in, rather than printed, so they don't wear off.

Dutch oven: If something has to go from the stove top to the oven, my cast-iron Dutch oven works for both and reduces extra dishes to wash.

Grill pan: I like to use a grill pan for steaks and grilled seafood.

Handheld mixer: I use my handheld mixer for almost everything because it's easy to clean up afterward. Mine is a KitchenAid because I like the all the attachments for it, like the dough hooks.

Kitchen shears: Remember how I don't like knives? I use kitchen shears to break down a whole raw chicken instead.

Large pot: I've got an aluminum Calphalon and a stainless-steel Cuisinart pot, and when it comes time to boil pasta, I use whichever is closest.

Liquid measuring cups: I use my two-cup Pyrex measuring cup for almost everything.

Masher: I use the kind of masher where the bottom looks like a squiggly line—but you can also mash with a whisk if you don't have a masher.

Liquid Measuring Cup versus Dry Measuring Cup

When cooking and baking, it's crucial to have both liquid and dry measuring cups. Depending on which cup you use to measure, you could end up with a different amount—and possibly mess up a recipe, especially when it comes to baking.

With liquid measurements, you want to use a cup that has extra room so that if you pour in too much, it doesn't spill, and you can pour off any excess through the spout. For dry measurements, you're likely to scoop them out of a container, so they fit the exact cup size—then after you scoop, you can brush any excess back into the container with a flat utensil and be left with the exact right amount. Using the right cup will help you get the precise measurement called for in the recipe so it turns out just like it should.

Measuring spoons: Like the measuring cups, I prefer steel and in a range from ⅛ teaspoon to 1 tablespoon. I don't like the ones that say "a pinch." That's not a standardized amount!

Mixing bowls: I like to use glass mixing bowls so I can see what I'm doing—if there's any spots or clumps that I missed.

Paring knife: Knives scare me, so I pretty much use my little paring knife for everything—and kitchen shears for anything else.

Potato peeler: Whatever kind of peeler you have works, though I prefer the long, thin kind—and always with a sharp end to scoop out the eyes.

Round cake pans: I use 9-inch Wilton cake pans; they usually come in a set of two for layer cakes.

Saucepan: My 12-inch nonstick is my everyday pan.

Sifter: Sifting takes the lumps out of flour before you use it, but if you don't have a sifter, you can just use your whisk to do the same thing.

Slow cooker: My slow cooker is a workhorse. I just throw everything in and don't have to babysit it. It's a Crock-Pot brand, just like my mom had, but the digital version so I can just set a timer, and then it automatically warms when finished cooking. Make sure that you are familiar with your slow cooker! Older slow cookers tend to run a tad bit hotter than newer ones, and this can affect your cooking time.

Spatula: Anything goes here, except for metal, which will scratch your nonstick pans. I prefer wood, but plastic is good too.

Springform pan: A high-quality nonstick springform pan is an essential for making cheesecake.

Stand mixer: I use my stand mixer mostly for big cakes or holidays. It's also a KitchenAid, and I like the tilt-head kind more than the bowl-lift, as it's easier to remove the bowl and clean.

Tongs: I use all-metal tongs for flipping things when I'm frying.

Whisk: In a whisk, metal is the best way to go.

Wooden spoons: Wood won't scratch your pots, and if you care for them properly, they last a long time. Be sure to wash your wooden spoons by hand, then dry them immediately.

Rise and Grind

Red Velvet Waffles   30

Cinnamon Toast Crunch French Toast   33

Southern Fried Cinnamon Apples   34

Ultimate Breakfast Sandwich   35

Egg, Sausage, and Potato Scramble   36

Soulful Breakfast Enchiladas   39

Steak and Cheese Omelette   41

Meat Lover's Quiche   42

Waffle Fried Chicken   45

Five-Cheese Hash Brown Casserole   47

Stuffed Hash Browns   48

Cheddar, Ham, and Grits Casserole   51

Red Velvet Waffles

I like red velvet everything and my son does too (see my Red Velvet Biscuits on page 95), so I went ahead and made waffles with red velvet batter. These fluffy, chocolatey waffles are festive for holidays, like Christmas and Valentine's Day, but they're also great for non-holidays. I'll pull out the waffle iron and make them on a random Sunday when I'm feeling extra. You can also change their color with a different food dye to make the waffles for other occasions.

MAKES 6 SERVINGS

2 cups all-purpose flour

¼ cup sugar

3 tablespoons unsweetened
  cocoa powder

2 teaspoons baking powder

2 teaspoons baking soda

1 teaspoon kosher salt

½ teaspoon ground nutmeg

1½ cups buttermilk

½ cup vegetable oil

2 large eggs

2 teaspoons vanilla extract

2 teaspoons red food coloring

1 teaspoon distilled white vinegar

Nonstick cooking spray

For topping (optional):

Southern Fried Cinnamon Apples
  (page 34)

Fresh fruit and whipped cream

Pure maple syrup

- In a large mixing bowl, combine the flour, sugar, cocoa, baking powder, baking soda, salt, and nutmeg. Whisk until well combined. Add the buttermilk, oil, and eggs, and whisk until well combined. Then add the vanilla, food coloring, and vinegar. Whisk the batter until smooth.

- Preheat a waffle iron until hot. Spray the waffle iron with nonstick cooking spray. Pour about ½ cup of the batter (check your waffle iron's instructions) onto the iron, and cook until the outer edges are nice and crisp, 5 to 6 minutes. Every waffle iron is different, but many have a light that indicates when the waffle is done. Transfer the waffles to a wire rack to cool for about a minute or so. Repeat until there is no more batter. Serve the waffles with the desired toppings.

Cinnamon Toast Crunch French Toast

I love to be creative when it comes to making breakfast. I make delicious French toast, and when I was thinking up this recipe, I decided that so many French toast recipes have great cinnamon flavor, so why not marry it with one of my favorite cereals? I started with the classic French toast, crushed Cinnamon Toast Crunch, and dipped the bread in it after I dunked it into the custard. You get that creamy interior with the bread and a crispy butter exterior. This French toast is really like nothing you've ever tried! It's perfect for dipping in maple syrup with a dollop of whipped cream. I like to change it up every once in a while, so feel free to use your favorite cereal and get creative with the bread. Stale brioche or French bread is perfect; just make sure to use thick and sturdy slices.

MAKES 6 SERVINGS

3 large eggs

2 cups half-and-half

2 teaspoons vanilla extract

2 teaspoons ground cinnamon

¼ teaspoon ground nutmeg

¼ cup salted butter, melted

12 slices thick-sliced bread

2 cups Cinnamon Toast Crunch cereal, crushed

Nonstick cooking spray

1½ cups whipped cream

2 cups fresh blueberries, strawberries, or blackberries

◆ In a large bowl or shallow dish, beat the eggs. Add the half-and-half, vanilla, cinnamon, and nutmeg, and stir. Pour in the melted butter and stir again.

◆ Place the cereal in a separate large bowl or shallow dish.

◆ Soak each slice of bread in the egg mixture for about 10 seconds. Coat each side of the bread with the crushed cereal, then set to the side.

◆ Spray a large skillet or griddle with nonstick spray, and place it over medium heat. Once the pan is hot, add the bread 2 to 4 slices at a time. Cook until nice and golden brown, 2 to 3 minutes per side. Repeat with the remaining slices. Serve with the whipped cream and berries on top.

Southern Fried Cinnamon Apples

Growing up, we always had apples in the house. (That might be because I would steal apples from the neighbors' trees . . . shhh.) My mom would bake or fry them with cinnamon to top pancakes, just like the Rooty Tooty Fresh 'N Fruity breakfast at IHOP! This recipe is my version of those apples. I still put them on pancakes but also waffles and oatmeal, or on the side of buttered biscuits, or sometimes just as a snack on their own.

MAKES 8 SERVINGS

5 large Granny Smith apples, peeled, cored, and sliced into ¼-inch wedges

2 tablespoons freshly squeezed lemon juice

3 tablespoons unsalted butter

3 tablespoons light brown sugar

2 tablespoons granulated sugar

1 teaspoon ground cinnamon

½ teaspoon ground nutmeg

◆ In a large mixing bowl, toss the apples with the lemon juice.

◆ In a large skillet, melt the butter over medium heat. Add the apples, both sugars, cinnamon, and nutmeg. Stir until the apples are coated with the sugar and spices. Simmer until the apples are nice and tender, 10 to 15 minutes. Serve and enjoy!

Ultimate Breakfast Sandwich

Breakfast sandwiches are always nostalgic for me. As Grandpa's girl, I got to try his breakfast sandwiches (because he didn't really know how to cook anything else), so I always think of him when I'm having one.

For this ultimate version, I add bacon *and* ham and put in on a bagel because I'm extra and bougie. You could use any sliced cheese, but I like the little kick that comes from pairing pepper jack with the bacon. Pile it all on with the egg and you really couldn't ask for a better breakfast on the run. This makes just one sandwich, but feel free to scale up the ingredients to make as many as you need to serve.

MAKES 1 SANDWICH	
1 plain bagel, split in half	1 slice thick-cut ham
2 teaspoons salted butter	1 large egg
2 slices thick-cut hickory-smoked bacon	2 slices pepper jack cheese

- Toast the bagel halves until golden brown, then spread with the butter.

- In a medium skillet over medium-high heat, add the bacon and cook, flipping once, until it's nice and crisp, about 5 minutes. Transfer the bacon to a paper-towel-lined plate, but leave the rendered fat in the skillet.

- Add the ham and cook each side for 2 to 3 minutes. Transfer the ham to the plate.

- Add the egg to the skillet and cook until it's over easy or over hard (whichever you prefer).

- While the egg is cooking, quickly assemble the sandwich: Top the bottom bagel half with the ham, followed by the bacon, then the cheese. Add the egg, then close the sandwich with the top bagel half and enjoy.

Egg, Sausage, and Potato Scramble

FAN FAVE!

When my husband and I go out for breakfast, his go-to order is scrambled eggs with cheese, plus sausage and a side of home fries. Instead of cooking each element separately, I decided to combine them all into one baked dish. Needless to say, this is his favorite. This dish is a great time-saver when you need to cook breakfast for a crowd. You can prep everything in advance and throw it together last minute as well. It also means you'll have fewer dishes to wash.

MAKES 6 SERVINGS

3 medium potatoes, peeled and diced

2 tablespoons extra-virgin olive oil

1 teaspoon seasoning salt or salt-free seasoning

1 teaspoon garlic powder

½ teaspoon ground black pepper

1 pound ground breakfast sausage

½ medium yellow onion, chopped

3 green onions, chopped, plus more for garnish

4 large eggs or 6 medium eggs, beaten

½ cup shredded cheese of choice

6 to 8 grape tomatoes, halved

◆ Preheat the oven to 350 degrees F.

◆ Place the potatoes in a 9-by-13-inch baking dish, and drizzle them with the olive oil. Sprinkle them all over with the seasoning salt, garlic powder, and pepper and toss until the potatoes are nicely coated. Bake for 15 to 20 minutes, or until the potatoes are fork-tender.

◆ Meanwhile, place the sausage in a large deep skillet over medium heat. Brown the sausage, breaking it up with a spatula, for about 5 minutes.

◆ When the potatoes are ready, add them to the sausage along with the yellow and green onions. Stir and cook until the sausage is cooked through and the yellow onions are translucent, 5 to 7 minutes.

◆ Pour the eggs into the skillet and stir until they are scrambled and well combined with the other ingredients. Sprinkle with ¼ cup of the cheese and stir it in.

◆ Once the eggs are cooked to your liking, remove the scramble from the skillet. Garnish with the tomatoes, remaining ¼ cup cheese, and additional green onions. Serve immediately and enjoy!

Soulful Breakfast Enchiladas

I grew up eating lots of Mexican food, and enchiladas for breakfast were a regular thing. Usually they were filled with sausage, so I thought why not try it with andouille? Instead of making home fries, I took a lazy shortcut and filled the enchiladas with frozen tater tots. This dish was a lifesaver when I was working twelve-hour days. I could make it in advance and heat it up for my son in the mornings.

MAKES ONE 9-BY-13-INCH PAN

For the enchiladas:
2 tablespoons vegetable oil, plus more for greasing
1 pound andouille sausage, diced
1 medium red bell pepper, diced
1 small red onion, sliced
5 large eggs, beaten
2 cups frozen tater tots
2 cups shredded Colby Jack cheese, divided
¼ cup mild salsa
2 teaspoons Creole seasoning
10 medium flour tortillas

For the sauce:
2 tablespoons unsalted butter
2 tablespoons vegetable oil
¼ cup all-purpose flour
1¾ cups chicken broth
½ cup sour cream
¼ cup mild salsa

Chopped fresh cilantro, for garnish

◆ Preheat the oven to 350 degrees F. Lightly grease a 9-by-13-inch baking dish with vegetable oil.

◆ To make the enchiladas, first drizzle the oil in a large skillet over medium-high heat. Add the sausage and cook for about 5 minutes, stirring occasionally. Toss in the bell pepper and onion. Cook, stirring occasionally, until softened, 2 to 3 minutes. Add the eggs and cook, scraping with a rubber spatula, until lightly scrambled, 3 to 4 minutes. Add the tater tots, 1½ cups of the cheese, salsa, and Creole seasoning and stir to combine. Set to the side.

CONTINUED

♥

- To make the sauce, in a large saucepan, heat the butter and oil over medium heat until the butter is melted, then stir to combine with the oil. Sprinkle in the flour and cook, whisking, until the raw flour smell is gone, 3 to 4 minutes. Slowly pour in the chicken broth, whisking until smooth. Bring to a boil, then turn the heat to low and simmer for a few minutes. Remove from the heat, add the sour cream and salsa, and stir.

- Spread ⅓ cup of the sauce on the bottom of the prepared baking dish.

- Divide the enchilada filling among the tortillas, then roll each one up like a burrito and place side by side, seam side down, in the baking dish. Top with the remaining sauce and remaining ½ cup cheese.

- Bake, uncovered, for 30 minutes, then place under the broiler until the cheese is golden. Garnish with the cilantro and dig in.

Steak and Cheese Omelette

Sometimes I think we can get into a rut where breakfast is concerned—sausage and bacon always seem to take center stage! Don't get me wrong: I love me some bacon and sausage, but sometimes it's such a nice surprise to use steak. When I fix steak for breakfast, it tastes a lot better to me. Instead of just steak with sunny-side-up eggs, I prefer my eggs incorporated with the meat. The result is this omelette loaded with cubed steak, mushrooms, and bell peppers. It's a big breakfast that's hearty enough for dinner.

MAKES 1 EXTRA-LARGE OMELETTE

3 large eggs
2 tablespoons half-and-half
½ teaspoon kosher salt
¼ teaspoon ground black pepper
1 tablespoon vegetable oil
1 tablespoon salted butter

¼ pound sirloin steak, cut into small cubes
2 tablespoons sliced mushrooms
1 tablespoon diced red bell pepper
¼ cup shredded cheddar cheese
1 tablespoon chopped green onion

♦ In a medium bowl, combine the eggs, half-and-half, salt, and black pepper. Whisk until well combined, then set to the side.

♦ In a large nonstick skillet, heat the oil and butter over medium-high heat. Add the steak and cook for 5 minutes, or until it reaches the desired doneness. Next, add the mushrooms and bell pepper. Cook until the peppers are tender, about 3 minutes. Transfer to a plate.

♦ Turn the heat to medium and pour the egg mixture into the skillet. Cook for 2 minutes, then lift the edges of the omelette with a spatula to let the raw egg run underneath the cooked parts until the omelette is fully cooked. Top with the steak mixture, sprinkle with the cheese, fold the omelette, and transfer it to a plate. Top with the green onion. Serve and enjoy!

Meat Lover's Quiche

You often see bacon or ham with cheese in a quiche. I decided to combine bacon *and* ham with breakfast sausage for this quiche. I got the idea from my husband, who loves to load up eggs with all the breakfast meats. When he sees the words "meat lover's" on a menu, he's bound to order that dish. You can prep this quiche in advance and bake it the next day. I like to serve it for special brunch occasions, like Easter.

MAKES ONE 9-INCH QUICHE

6 large eggs, beaten
¾ cup half-and-half
½ pound ground breakfast sausage, cooked and crumbled
½ pound hickory-smoked bacon, cooked and crumbled
½ cup diced ham

1½ cups shredded Colby Jack cheese
½ cup chopped green onions
½ cup diced red bell pepper
2 teaspoons seasoning salt
½ teaspoon ground black pepper
1 store-bought deep-dish pastry shell, frozen

◆ Preheat the oven to 375 degrees F.

◆ In a large mixing bowl, whisk the eggs with the half-and-half. Add the sausage, bacon, ham, cheese, green onions, bell pepper, and seasoning salt, and pepper. Stir to combine, then pour the mixture into the frozen pastry shell.

◆ Bake for 30 to 35 minutes, or until the crust is golden brown and the filling is just set. Remove from the oven and let sit for 10 minutes before serving.

Waffle Fried Chicken

My family has been eating chicken and waffles *way* before it became popular. My grandma was the genius behind this. Grandma was the head cook at a nursing home back in the day. One evening, they were supposed to make fried chicken. However, they were short on flour. My grandma, wonderful cook that she was, quickly thought up a new recipe: "waffle fried chicken." She replaced the missing flour with waffle mix, and everyone loved it. This dish became a family favorite. Today, everyone in my family has their own twist, but of course I make it the best! Let me show you how it's done!

MAKES 6 TO 8 SERVINGS

For the brine:
8 cups cold water
¼ cup sugar
2 tablespoons kosher salt

For the chicken:
2 pounds chicken wings, cleaned (see Cleaning Poultry 101 on page 140) and separated into flats and drumettes

½ cup hot sauce
2 teaspoons seasoning salt
1 teaspoon ground black pepper
½ teaspoon cayenne pepper
1½ cups waffle mix
½ cup self-rising flour
2½ cups vegetable oil, for deep-frying
Maple syrup and hot sauce, for serving (optional)

- In a large mixing bowl, combine all the brine ingredients, stirring until the sugar and salt dissolve. Place the chicken in a separate large bowl, then pour the brine all over it. Cover the bowl and refrigerate for 6 to 8 hours or overnight, then drain. Once you drain the brine, don't rinse the wings.

- Pour the hot sauce all over the chicken and toss to coat. Next, sprinkle the chicken with the seasoning salt, black pepper, and cayenne. Toss to coat.

- In a large paper or plastic bag, combine the waffle mix and flour and shake the bag until they are well incorporated.

CONTINUED

- Add a few wings at a time to the flour mixture. Shake the bag until the wings are well coated, then remove them from the bag and set aside on a plate. Repeat with the remaining wings. Let the chicken sit for 10 minutes before frying.

- Pour the oil into a deep fryer or a large deep frying pan, and heat over medium heat to 350 to 360 degrees F. Start adding a few wings at a time. Be sure not to over-crowd the pan! Fry one side of each piece, then flip over and fry the other side until the chicken is cooked through and golden brown all over, about 7 minutes total.

- Remove the chicken with tongs and place it on a paper-towel-lined baking sheet or plate to cool slightly. Repeat with the remaining chicken.

- Serve the wings with maple syrup and hot sauce.

Five-Cheese Hash Brown Casserole

Everybody loves hash browns, but nobody really wants to clean, peel, and grate all those potatoes! My simple solution is to use frozen hash browns—they are a game changer! All you have to do is mix them with eggs and cheese, then bake it all in a casserole. It's a crowd-friendly dish that still feels luxurious because of all the melty cheese. I like to make this casserole for Christmas morning. You can mix it up the night before to save time in the morning when you want to be opening presents. Keep it in mind for your family gatherings and special brunches.

MAKES ONE 9-BY-13-INCH PAN

Vegetable oil, for greasing

4 cups frozen shredded hash brown potatoes, thawed

7 large eggs, lightly beaten

2 cups shredded sharp cheddar cheese

1 cup shredded Colby Jack cheese

1 cup shredded mozzarella cheese

1 cup shredded Havarti cheese

1 cup shredded Muenster cheese

2 teaspoons garlic powder

2 teaspoons seasoning salt

1½ teaspoons ground black pepper

◆ Preheat the oven to 375 degrees F. Lightly grease a 9-by-13-inch baking dish.

◆ In a large mixing bowl, combine all the ingredients and mix well. Transfer to the prepared baking dish.

◆ Bake, uncovered, for 40 to 45 minutes, or until the hash browns are nice and golden brown. Remove from the oven and let sit for 5 to 10 minutes before serving.

Stuffed Hash Browns

Back when waffling every possible kind of frozen food went viral, someone tagged me in a video for waffled frozen hash browns. I was really delighted by the idea. The hash browns developed all these nooks and crannies and looked so delicious. Best of all, the method was so easy.

I took that concept a step further by adding a layer of cheesy scrambled eggs and breakfast sausage between the hash browns. That way you get an all-in-one meal that cooks right in a waffle iron. You don't even have to flip the hash browns. It might be worth getting a waffle iron just for this recipe.

MAKES 4 TO 6 SERVINGS

1 pound ground breakfast sausage
1 medium red bell pepper, diced
6 green onions, diced
9 large eggs, divided
1¼ cups shredded pepper jack cheese
1 cup shredded sharp cheddar cheese

4 cups frozen shredded hash brown
    potatoes, thawed
Nonstick cooking spray
2 tablespoons butter
Sour cream and chopped fresh
    parsley, for garnish

- Heat a large nonstick skillet over medium heat until hot. Add the sausage and cook, breaking up the meat, until browned, about 7 minutes. Toss in the bell pepper and green onions. Cook, stirring occasionally, until the peppers are softened, about 3 minutes. Pour off the excess oil from the skillet.

- In a medium bowl, lightly beat 7 of the eggs, then add them to the skillet. Stir and cook until the eggs are just set. Remove the pan from the heat and sprinkle both cheeses over the eggs, then fold in.

- In a large mixing bowl, lightly beat the remaining 2 eggs, then add the hash browns and mix until well combined.

- Preheat a waffle iron until hot, then spray with nonstick cooking spray. Add a layer of the hash browns, then some of the scrambled egg mixture, then top off with another layer of hash browns.

- Close the waffle iron and cook for 4 minutes, or until the hash browns are nice and golden brown. Transfer the stuffed hash brown to a plate, top with some sour cream and chopped parsley, and serve. Repeat with the remaining ingredients.

Cheddar, Ham, and Grits Casserole

I love hosting brunch events. One of my go-to recipes would have to be this ham and grits casserole. It's one of those casseroles that you can make ahead and pop in the oven right before serving. It's the perfect combination of creamy grits, cheese, and diced ham. If you're not thrilled about pork, you can always replace the ham with diced turkey bacon or crumbled turkey sausage.

MAKES ONE 9-BY-13-INCH CASSEROLE

Vegetable oil, for greasing
3 cups chicken broth
2 cups water
1 cup half-and-half
2 teaspoons seasoning salt
½ teaspoon garlic powder
½ teaspoon onion powder
½ teaspoon ground black pepper
2 cups quick grits
2 cups diced ham
2 cups shredded cheddar cheese
2 large eggs, lightly beaten
½ cup (1 stick) salted butter

◆ Preheat the oven to 350 degrees F. Lightly grease a 9-by-13-inch baking dish.

◆ In a large pot over medium-high heat, combine the chicken broth, water, and half-and-half and bring to a boil. Sprinkle in the seasoning salt, garlic powder, onion powder, and pepper and stir.

◆ Slowly add the grits to the pot, whisking the liquid to remove any lumps. Turn the heat down to low and cook for 15 minutes, stirring occasionally. Remove from the heat and let the grits cool for 15 minutes.

◆ Next, add the ham, cheese, eggs, and butter to the grits and stir until well combined. Transfer to the prepared baking dish.

◆ Bake for 45 minutes, or until the top of the casserole is nice and golden brown. Remove from the oven and let the casserole sit for 15 minutes before serving.

Wanna Be Startin' Somethin'

Turnip Greens and Artichoke Au Gratin Dip   55

Voodoo Dip   56

Cajun Blooming Onions   59

Creole Loaded Potato Skins   61

Bacon-Wrapped Stuffed Jalapeños   65

Loaded Baked Oysters   66

Grilled Creole Shrimp Cocktails   67

Fried Salmon Bites   71

Creole Crab Cakes with Sweet Chili Sauce   72

Poached Garlic Crab Legs   74

Royal Wings   75

Fried Chicken Gizzards   76

Fried Chicken Sliders   79

Boudin Balls   80

Southern Meat Pies with Creole Chimichurri   82

Turnip Greens and Artichoke Au Gratin Dip

This is my spin on the traditional spinach and artichoke dip. Instead of spinach, I love to use turnip greens. Shhh, don't tell anyone, but I think I like a turnip green better than a collard—and I *love* my collard greens! Look for them next to collard and mustard greens in the produce section. The smoked gouda adds another layer of flavor to the hot dip. It's a crowd pleaser on game day or for any gathering.

MAKES 6 SERVINGS

6 to 8 slices bacon
1½ cups chopped turnip greens
⅓ cup chopped artichokes
   (I use frozen)
2 tablespoons chopped red
   bell pepper
2 garlic cloves, minced
2 tablespoons all-purpose flour
½ cup heavy cream

6 ounces sour cream
6 ounces cream cheese, at
   room temperature
¼ cup chopped green onions
1 teaspoon minced fresh thyme leaves
⅔ cup shredded smoked Gouda
⅔ cup shredded creamy Havarti
Chips, veggie sticks, or toasted bread,
   for serving

♦ Preheat the broiler.

♦ Place a large skillet over medium heat, add the bacon, and cook, flipping once, until it's nice and crisp, about 5 minutes. Remove the bacon from the skillet and set aside to cool, but leave the rendered fat. Crumble or chop the bacon.

♦ Pour 2 tablespoons of the bacon fat into a medium pan (reserve the rest for another use) and place over medium heat. Toss in the turnip greens and cook, stirring occasionally, for about 5 minutes. Stir in the artichokes and bell pepper. Add the garlic and cook, stirring, for 1 minute. Sprinkle in the flour and cook, stirring, until the raw flour smell is gone, about 3 minutes. Add the heavy cream, sour cream, and cream cheese and stir. Add the bacon, green onions, and thyme.

♦ Transfer the dip to a medium baking dish or several smaller baking dishes—make sure they are broiler safe! Top with the shredded cheese. Broil until the top of the dip bubbles and starts to brown, 2 to 3 minutes.

♦ Let the dip cool for 5 to 10 minutes before digging in. Serve with chips, veggie sticks, or toasted bread.

Voodoo Dip

♥

Why do I call it voodoo dip? Because it's Creole-inspired, with lots of spice and jalapeño. It's basically queso, but instead of serving it with tortilla chips, try crusty French bread—toasted or not. This dip is simple to make, and it brings out my love for Louisiana and the French Quarter.

It's also best served hot, so set it out ASAP. Here is a Cousin Rosie tip: any dips that you don't want getting cold, serve them up in a slow cooker on the warm setting. You'd be surprised how long the dip stays creamy and delicious instead of getting chilly too fast. This method is great for any party or gathering.

MAKES 12 SERVINGS

2 tablespoons salted butter

¼ cup chopped red bell pepper

¼ cup chopped green onions

1 medium jalapeño, minced

3 garlic cloves, minced

1 (12-ounce) can evaporated milk

8 ounces cream cheese

½ cup whole milk, divided

8 ounces shredded sharp cheddar cheese

8 ounces shredded pepper jack cheese

½ pound chopped cooked shrimp meat

1 teaspoon red pepper flakes

1 teaspoon Creole seasoning

½ teaspoon onion powder

Crusty bread and tortilla chips, for serving

◆ Melt the butter in a medium skillet over medium heat. Toss in the bell pepper, green onions, jalapeño, and garlic, and cook, stirring, for 2 minutes.

◆ Next, add the evaporated milk and cream cheese, and stir until the cream cheese is melted. Reduce the heat to low and pour in ¼ cup of the whole milk. Whisk until well combined. Add the shredded cheeses, and whisk until everything is well incorporated. Stir in the remaining ¼ cup milk to thin out the dip.

◆ Finally, fold the shrimp meat, red pepper flakes, Creole seasoning, and onion powder into the dip, then transfer it to a serving dish. Serve immediately with crusty bread and tortilla chips.

Cajun Blooming Onions

These are like the Bloomin' Onion from Outback Steakhouse but much cheaper and I get to flavor them the way I want—with Cajun seasoning. They're fun to serve for movie nights and game days. Put sweet onions on your grocery list; they are larger and milder than a regular yellow onion. We are known for Walla Walla sweets out here in the Pacific Northwest, but any sweet onion will do. If you can't find them, then a yellow onion soaked in ice water for fifteen minutes will do just fine. You probably already have the other ingredients to make this recipe. I use regular-size onions because I have no idea where Outback gets those steroid onions. How do they get so big?

MAKES 6 SERVINGS

For the sauce:
- ¾ cup mayonnaise
- ½ cup sour cream
- 4½ tablespoons ketchup
- 4½ tablespoons creamy horseradish
- 2 tablespoons Dijon mustard
- 2 teaspoons freshly squeezed lemon juice
- 2 teaspoons Cajun seasoning
- 1½ teaspoons paprika
- 1 teaspoon Tabasco or your choice of hot sauce

For the onions:
- 2 large eggs
- 1 cup whole milk
- 2 cups all-purpose flour
- 2½ teaspoons Cajun seasoning
- 2 teaspoons garlic powder
- 2 teaspoons onion powder
- 2 teaspoons seasoning salt
- 1 teaspoon ground black pepper
- 3 medium sweet onions
- Vegetable oil (I use corn oil), for deep-frying

♦ First, make the sauce. In a small bowl, combine all the sauce ingredients and stir until well combined. Set aside.

♦ Next, in a large mixing bowl, whisk the eggs and milk. In a separate large mixing bowl, combine the flour, Cajun seasoning, garlic powder, onion powder, seasoning salt, and pepper. Whisk until well combined, then set to the side.

♦ To prepare the onions, peel them and trim off the tops. Hold an onion trimmed side down. Starting from the top, make a vertical cut through the center three-fourths of the way down to keep the bottom intact. Repeat all around the top every ¼ inch or so to create the blooming onion "petals." Do the same to the remaining onions.

CONTINUED

◆ Fan out the petals, then coat each onion with the seasoned flour, followed by the egg mixture, then again with the seasoned flour until nicely coated.

◆ Pour 3 to 4 inches of vegetable oil into a large pot. Heat over medium-high heat until the oil is 350 degrees F, or until it begins to shimmer and dance a bit across the top.

◆ Deep-fry the onions, flipping once, until golden brown, about 7 minutes. Remove the onions from the oil and place them on a paper-towel-lined plate. Let them cool until safe to eat, then serve with the sauce.

Creole Loaded Potato Skins

My chore as a child was to peel potatoes with a knife. Of course, I ended up taking off too much flesh with the peel so my mom, being resourceful, froze the trimmings to turn into fried potato skins baked with cheese. She was not going to waste all that good potato! To this day, I love potato skins, but the usual toppings kind of bore me. I decided to spice mine up with some Creole seasoning, andouille sausage, and pepper jack cheese. These are a great app for parties, especially around Christmastime because of the green and red garnishes.

MAKES 12 POTATO SKINS

6 medium russet potatoes, scrubbed
2 tablespoons salted butter, melted
2 teaspoons Creole seasoning
8 slices bacon
2 andouille sausage links, diced
¾ cup shredded sharp cheddar cheese

¾ cup shredded pepper jack cheese
¼ cup chopped green onions
¼ cup chopped red bell pepper
¼ cup chopped fresh cilantro
2 garlic cloves, minced
¾ cup sour cream

- ◆ Preheat the oven to 400 degrees F.

- ◆ Pierce each potato a few times with a fork, then place them on a baking sheet lined with parchment paper. Brush the potatoes with the melted butter, then sprinkle with the Creole seasoning. Bake for 50 to 55 minutes, then remove from the oven and let cool. Leave the oven on.

- ◆ Meanwhile, in a large skillet over medium heat, add the bacon and cook, flipping once, until it's nice and crisp, about 5 minutes. Remove the bacon from the skillet and set aside to cool, but leave the rendered fat. Crumble or chop the bacon.

- ◆ Return the skillet to medium heat, then add the andouille sausage and cook until brown, about 6 minutes. Transfer the sausage to a small plate and set aside.

CONTINUED

* Once they are cool enough to handle, cut the potatoes in half lengthwise. Scoop out the flesh (save it for another use, if desired), leaving about a ¼-inch rim of potato all around the inside of the skins. Place the potato skins cut side down on the baking sheet and bake for 8 minutes.

* Remove the baking sheet from the oven but leave the oven on. Flip the potato skins over so they're cut side up. Fill the skins with the sausage and both cheeses. Bake for 2 minutes, or until the cheese has melted.

* Remove from the oven and top the potato skins with the bacon, green onions, bell pepper, cilantro, and garlic. Add a little sour cream on top and then serve.

Bacon-Wrapped Stuffed Jalapeños

I've always loved jalapeño poppers, but once you get beyond the breaded coating, things get kind of boring, and I want food that's exciting! So I decided to wrap the jalapeños in bacon, which gives you that salty-sweet smokiness. This dish is actually easier than making traditional poppers because it requires only three ingredients and no frying at all. People go crazy for this app when I serve it on game days, so be sure to make enough to go around. If you do want to jazz things up, add some shrimp or crab to the filling, like I do for the holidays.

MAKES 12 STUFFED JALAPEÑO HALVES

---

6 jumbo jalapeños   1 pound bacon
8 ounces cream cheese, softened

◆ Preheat the oven to 375 degrees F. Line a baking sheet with aluminum foil for easier cleanup, then fit a wire rack on top.

◆ Cut off the jalapeño stems and discard them, then cut each jalapeño in half lengthwise. Using a small spoon, scoop out all the seeds and discard them. Rinse the jalapeños under cool water to help remove any stubborn seeds stuck inside.

◆ Using the same spoon, stuff the jalapeño halves with cream cheese, then carefully wrap each half with bacon to completely cover the cream cheese.

◆ Place the jalapeños, cream cheese side up, on the prepared wire rack. Bake for 25 to 30 minutes, or until the bacon is nice and crisp, then serve hot.

Loaded Baked Oysters

This recipe is a riff on the oysters Rockefeller I had at the Golden Steer Steakhouse in Las Vegas. Instead of topping oysters with buttered spinach and bread crumbs, I tried it with some leftover creamed spinach. Then I took the dish further by adding lobster meat and mozzarella. Might as well go all out! The way the topping bubbles up in the oven is just magic. I like the way oysters taste with red onions, but if the flavor is too strong for you, substitute green onions or leave them out.

MAKES 24 BAKED OYSTERS ON THE HALF SHELLS

2 dozen large raw oysters, shucked and on the half shell

2½ teaspoons Creole seasoning

1 teaspoon red pepper flakes

1 batch Creamed Spinach with Bacon (page 166)

½ cup minced cooked lobster meat

¼ cup shredded mozzarella cheese

¼ cup diced red onion

Hot sauce, for serving

---

* Preheat the oven to 400 degrees F.

* Line a rimmed baking sheet with dry rice, rock salt, or crumpled aluminum foil. Nestle the oysters in theirs shells on the pan, spacing them evenly. Sprinkle with the Creole seasoning and red pepper. Top the oysters with the creamed spinach, followed by the lobster meat, then the mozzarella. Sprinkle the onions on top.

* Bake for 8 to 10 minutes, or until the mozzarella is bubbling. Remove from the oven and let cool slightly. Serve with hot sauce.

Grilled Creole Shrimp Cocktails

There's something about adding shrimp to my appetizer menu that makes me feel bad and bougie. I don't know what it is, but when I have guests over and I serve them shrimp, I just feel like I'm earning bragging rights. This shrimp cocktail happens to be my golden dish when I want to impress. When you grill the shrimp, instead of just boiling or steaming them, they take on a whole new depth of flavor. Everyone loves this app; little do they know it takes just a few minutes to whip up.

The hardest part about this recipe is remembering to make it ahead of time. This recipe *must* be made in advance and refrigerated for a minimum of six hours before serving. The shrimp must be chilled, and you must let the cocktail sauce sit in the refrigerator so that all the flavors can marry for the best damn cocktail sauce you'll ever make and have. Are you ready to become bad and bougie? Well, then get this made!

MAKES 12 SERVINGS

For the shrimp:
3 pounds jumbo shrimp, peeled and deveined, tails left on
3 tablespoons extra-virgin olive oil
1 tablespoon Creole seasoning
2 teaspoons dried parsley flakes
Nonstick cooking spray

For the cocktail sauce:
1 cup ketchup
½ cup regular (not sweet) chili sauce
2 tablespoons minced red onion
2 tablespoons creamy horseradish sauce
2 tablespoons freshly squeezed lemon juice
1 tablespoon chopped fresh cilantro
1 tablespoon Tabasco or your choice of hot sauce
2 teaspoons minced garlic
2 teaspoons Worcestershire sauce
2 teaspoons Creole seasoning
1 teaspoon seafood seasoning
1 teaspoon red pepper flakes

CONTINUED

- Place the shrimp in a large bowl, then drizzle with the olive oil. Sprinkle with the Creole seasoning and parsley, and use your hands to toss the shrimp until it's well coated.

- Spray a large grill pan with nonstick spray and set it over medium heat until it's nice and hot. Start adding the shrimp, one layer at a time, and grill until they turn pink and look cooked through, about 2 minutes on each side. Remove the shrimp to a plate and let cool. Repeat until all the shrimp are cooked.

- While the shrimp is cooling, make the cocktail sauce. Combine all the sauce ingredients in a medium mixing bowl and mix until well combined. Cover the bowl with plastic wrap.

- Refrigerate the shrimp and sauce for at least 6 hours. Serve them together at your next party!

NOTE:

Make it fancy by serving these in cute cups. Simply add the sauce to the cups, then add the shrimp around the rim of the cup!

Fried Salmon Bites

Here in the Pacific Northwest, we absolutely love our salmon! We have tried just about every recipe you can think of using this fish. People love baked salmon, blackened salmon, grilled . . . but fried? Not so much. I decided I must come up with a delicious fried salmon bite. In my first book I perfected fried catfish, but I love just about every fried fish, so salmon was owed its time in the spotlight.

The result is a simple recipe that is extremely tasty and uses just a few ingredients. Yellow mustard adds a lot of flavor and helps bind the coating to the fish. These are great on their own, but you can absolutely serve them with a tasty dipping sauce like tartar or comeback sauce. The spicy tartar on my Spicy Catfish and Oyster Po'boys (page 118) would be fantastic.

MAKES 4 TO 6 SERVINGS

2 pounds skinless salmon fillets, cut into bite-size pieces	2 teaspoons lemon pepper
¼ cup yellow mustard	2 teaspoons seafood seasoning (I use RosaMae's Seafood Magic)
1 cup self-rising flour	½ teaspoon cayenne pepper
½ cup yellow cornmeal	2 to 2½ cups vegetable oil, for frying

◆ Coat the salmon pieces with the mustard, then set to the side.

◆ In a large bowl, combine the flour, cornmeal, lemon pepper, seafood seasoning, and cayenne. Mix well.

◆ Toss the salmon with the flour mixture to coat. Let the fish sit for about 5 minutes so the flour can adhere.

◆ In a large skillet, heat the oil to 360 to 370 degrees F. Working in batches to avoid overcrowding, carefully add the fish and fry until golden brown, 5 to 6 minutes. Remove from the oil and let the salmon drain on a paper-towel-lined plate or baking sheet until cool enough to eat.

Creole Crab Cakes with Sweet Chili Sauce

Because of my Louisiana roots, I like to add a Creole touch to pretty much any dish. For these crab cakes, I add lots of Creole seasoning, red bell peppers, and a bit of cilantro (which you can omit). I use a combo of lump crab and shredded crab for a better texture. The white bread is used as a binder to help hold everything together. It also takes on the flavor of the other ingredients, so you don't have to worry about tasting regular ol' bread while biting into these delicious crab cakes.

MAKES 4 TO 6 SERVINGS

For the sauce:
6 tablespoons warm water, divided
¼ cup distilled white vinegar
¼ cup sugar
2 garlic cloves, finely minced
1 tablespoon sambal oelek
2 teaspoons soy sauce
1 teaspoon salt-free Creole seasoning
½ teaspoon red pepper flakes
½ teaspoon cornstarch

For the crab cakes:
1 pound crabmeat (combination of
   lump and shredded)
6 slices white bread, crusts
   removed, cubed

¼ cup diced red bell pepper
¼ cup chopped green onions
⅔ cup mayonnaise
2 large eggs, at room temperature
2 tablespoons yellow mustard
2 teaspoons hot sauce (optional)
2 teaspoons Creole seasoning
1 teaspoon chopped fresh
   cilantro (optional)
1 teaspoon Old Bay Seasoning or your
   choice of seafood seasoning
½ teaspoon ground black pepper

Vegetable oil, for frying

- To make the sauce, in a small saucepan over medium heat, combine 4 tablespoons of the water, the vinegar, sugar, garlic, sambal, soy sauce, Creole seasoning, and red pepper flakes. Bring to a simmer. Whisk the remaining 2 tablespoons water and cornstarch in a small bowl, then stir it into the sauce to thicken. Cook for 1 more minute.

- To make the crab cakes, add all the ingredients except the oil to a large mixing bowl, and mix until everything is well combined. Form into 4 to 6 patties.

- Lightly oil a large skillet and place it over medium heat. Working in batches if necessary, add the crab cakes in a single layer and cook until nice and golden, 3 to 5 minutes per side. Serve with the sweet chili sauce on the side for dipping.

Poached Garlic Crab Legs

My son is a crab fiend. He can sit and crack crabs all day. If someone cracks the shells for him, even better. For this dish, I remove the crabmeat from the shells and poach it in seasoned butter. That way you don't have to dip the crab in butter at the table. For an extra-special brunch treat, serve the crab over grits.

MAKES 4 TO 6 SERVINGS

3 to 4 pounds king crab legs (or use whatever crab legs you can find)	2 teaspoons seafood seasoning
½ cup (1 stick) salted butter	1 teaspoon lemon pepper
2 tablespoons extra-virgin olive oil	1 teaspoon red pepper flakes
2 teaspoons minced garlic	¼ cup chopped fresh parsley
	1 large lemon, sliced into thin wedges

- Crack open all the crab legs; carefully remove the crabmeat and place on a plate. Discard the shells.

- Next, toss the butter into a large pan and drizzle in the olive oil. Turn the heat to medium and let the butter melt. Add the garlic, seafood seasoning, lemon pepper, and red pepper flakes. Stir until everything is well incorporated.

- Add the crabmeat to the pan and cook for 5 minutes, spooning the seasoned butter all over the crabmeat.

- Transfer the crabmeat to a deep platter, pour the butter all over, and garnish with the parsley and lemon wedges.

Royal Wings

I originally set out to make my friend's Hennessy wings until I saw the price of Hennessy at the liquor store . . . So, I went with Crown Royal instead, and that's how these wings got their name. (You can also buy a Crown Royal substitute or use whatever dark liquor you might have in your cupboard to save even more money.) A little sweet, savory, and spicy, these wings have an addictive combo of flavors that you can't get from any ol' restaurant. Make this dish for special occasions when you want to impress people, because whisky ain't cheap, y'all!

MAKES 8 SERVINGS

For the wings:
Nonstick cooking spray
4 pounds chicken wings, cleaned (see Cleaning Poultry 101 on page 140) and separated into flats and drumettes
2 tablespoons vegetable oil
2 tablespoons seasoning salt
2 tablespoons cornstarch

For the sauce:
1½ cups hickory barbecue sauce
½ cup Crown Royal whisky
½ cup dark brown sugar
½ cup honey
¼ cup minced onion
3 garlic cloves, minced
1 large jalapeño, diced (optional, for heat)
Zest of 1 large orange
Zest of 1 large lemon

- Preheat the oven to 400 degrees F. Spray a large rimmed baking sheet with nonstick spray.

- Place the wings in a large mixing bowl and drizzle with the vegetable oil. Next, sprinkle the seasoning salt and cornstarch over the chicken, then toss with your hands. Place the wings on the prepared baking sheet and bake for 30 minutes, or until the chicken is crisp and golden brown.

- Meanwhile, in a large saucepan, combine all the sauce ingredients and stir to incorporate. Cook over medium heat until the sauce thickens, about 5 minutes.

- Remove the baking sheet from the oven, then pour the sauce all over the wings so they're evenly coated. Bake for 10 more minutes, or until the sauce is nice and sticky. Plate the wings and enjoy!

Fried Chicken Gizzards

I used to go to a place in my area famous for fried chicken. What made them special was they fried all parts of the bird. My favorite items to order were the fried chicken livers and gizzards. I love the dark meat taste and chewy texture of gizzards. When fried right, the gizzards are nice and crispy on the outside, and tender to the middle. I like my gizzards with lots of hot sauce and served with fries. If you've never tried these, you must! Serve as an app or main—I like them either way.

MAKES 4 SERVINGS

For the brine:
8 cups cold water
¼ cup sugar
2 tablespoons kosher salt

For the gizzards:
4 pounds chicken gizzards, cleaned
   (see Cleaning Poultry 101 on
   page 140)

½ cup mild hot sauce, plus more
   for serving
2¼ cups all-purpose flour
¼ cup cornstarch
1½ tablespoons onion powder
1½ tablespoons garlic powder
3½ teaspoons seasoning salt
2 teaspoons paprika
1 teaspoon dried thyme
4 cups vegetable oil, for deep-frying

- First, make the brine. In a large mixing bowl, combine the cold water, sugar, and kosher salt, stirring until the sugar and salt dissolve.

- Place the gizzards in a large bowl or airtight container. Add the brine to cover the gizzards. Cover and refrigerate overnight or a minimum of 6 hours.

- Drain the gizzards and transfer them to a large bowl. Add the hot sauce and toss to coat.

- Next, combine the flour, cornstarch, onion powder, garlic powder, seasoning salt, paprika, and thyme in a gallon freezer bag. Toss in the gizzards and shake the bag until they are well coated.

- Remove the gizzards and shake off any excess flour. Let sit for about 15 minutes before frying to ensure that the coating sticks.

- Pour 2 inches of the oil into a large deep skillet and heat it to 375 degrees F.

- Working in batches so you don't overcrowd the skillet, carefully fry the gizzards, flipping once, until completely cooked through and golden brown, 10 to 15 minutes. Transfer them to a paper-towel-lined plate. Serve with lots of hot sauce!

Fried Chicken Sliders

Remember the Popeyes chicken sandwich craze a while back? I wanted to make fried chicken sliders and prove to my son I could make them even better! It wasn't even a question in my mind that mine were going to be tastier. I set out to make these appetizer size. Sometimes you gotta get in and make bite-size food so you can enjoy more than one. I brine the chicken in buttermilk to get it nice and tender and help flavor it; make sure you don't rinse off the buttermilk—just shake off the excess. That buttermilk is the secret to what makes the crust so delicious on the chicken. I think we could all guess that my son did say it's better than Popeyes. I know my cousins will agree as well!

MAKES 12 SLIDERS

4 thin boneless, skinless chicken breasts (about 2 pounds), cleaned (see Cleaning Poultry 101 on page 140) and trimmed of fat

4 cups buttermilk

1½ cups all-purpose flour

1 tablespoon seasoning salt

2 teaspoons Cajun seasoning

2 teaspoons poultry seasoning

2 teaspoons garlic powder

2 teaspoons onion powder

1½ teaspoons ground black pepper

3 cups vegetable oil, for deep-frying

12 slider buns

Mayonnaise, for the buns

Dill pickle chips, for serving

◆ Cut each chicken breast into thirds (you will need 12 pieces total) and place in a large bowl. Add the buttermilk, cover, and refrigerate for 3 to 4 hours.

◆ Drain the chicken—but *do not* rinse it—and set to the side.

◆ In a gallon plastic bag, combine the flour, seasoning salt, Cajun seasoning, poultry seasoning, garlic powder, onion powder, and black pepper. Shake the bag until everything is well combined.

◆ Toss the chicken pieces in the bag, and shake until they are well coated. Let sit for 10 minutes.

◆ Pour the vegetable oil into a large skillet and heat over medium heat to 360 degrees F. Deep-fry the chicken until golden brown, 10 to 15 minutes. Remove the chicken from the oil and place it on a paper-towel-lined plate.

◆ Spread mayonnaise on the slider buns, then place a piece of chicken and a few pickle chips on each bottom bun. Serve and enjoy!

Boudin Balls

Many of you know that I got my start on YouTube, and there weren't many cooking channels at the time—I think the most popular one was Chef John's. I was a huge fan of his. I loved his humor and his approach to cooking. One of my favorite recipes from Chef John was the boudin balls. To be honest, before trying his recipe, I had never made blood sausage. I just ate it when it was available. I tried his recipe and was really impressed! I used it as a blueprint for my own. The outcome was amazing, and it's one of the many dishes that I make as a holiday appetizer. Boudin balls are like boudin sausage: pork, liver, and rice. Really popular in Creole recipes, you'll find them served up around Mardi Gras. Note that this one has to be prepared the night before serving, so be sure to keep that in mind!

MAKES 14 TO 16 SERVINGS

¾ pounds boneless pork shoulder, cut into 1–inch cubes

6 ounces chicken livers, rinsed and trimmed

1 medium red onion, diced

4 large jalapeños, diced

2 stalks celery, diced

6 garlic cloves, minced

2 tablespoons Creole seasoning

2½ teaspoons ground black pepper

2 teaspoons kosher salt

2 teaspoons dried thyme

4 cups cooked long-grain white rice

½ cup chopped green onions

1 cup all-purpose flour

2 teaspoons garlic salt

2 large eggs, beaten

1 cup plain dried bread crumbs

2½ cups vegetable oil, for frying

* In a large bowl, combine the pork, chicken livers, onion, jalapeños, celery, garlic, Creole seasoning, pepper, salt, and thyme. Stir all the ingredients, then cover the bowl and refrigerate overnight.

* Place the boudin mixture in a large pot, then pour in 3 cups of water. Bring to a boil over medium heat. Reduce the heat to low and simmer for about 1½ hours. Remove the pot from the heat and drain, reserving the liquid for later.

* Transfer the boudin mixture to a food processor and pulse a few times until well blended. If you don't have a food processor, mince the meat finely with a knife. Transfer it to a large mixing bowl, add the rice and green onions, and stir until well combined.

- Next, start adding the reserved liquid, a little at a time, until the boudin mixture has a thick, pasty texture. Cover with plastic wrap and refrigerate for at least 2 hours.

- After the time has passed, pour the vegetable oil into a large skillet and heat it to 360 degrees F. While the oil is heating, roll the boudin mixture into 1-inch balls.

- Once the balls are rolled, set out the coating ingredients: In a medium bowl, combine the flour with the garlic salt and stir. In another medium bowl, add the beaten eggs. And in a third bowl, add the bread crumbs.

- To coat each boudin ball, start with the flour mixture, then shake off the excess. Next, carefully dip the ball in the beaten egg, then coat with the bread crumbs. Place on a baking sheet, then repeat with the remaining balls.

- Working in batches to avoid overcrowding the skillet, fry the boudin balls in the oil until golden brown all over, 5 to 7 minutes. Remove the boudin balls to a paper-towel-lined plate. Serve and enjoy!

Southern Meat Pies with Creole Chimichurri

I love Southern meat pies. They're like potpies, but stuffed with mainly meat and you don't need a fork! These delicious hand pies are eaten like a burger, so all you need are napkins. I make my meat pies pretty simple. I find that 80/20 is the best ratio of lean-to-fat beef for the filling. It keeps the pies moist—and the last thing you want to do is make dry meat pies, because folks will talk about you! Along with the beef, I also add spicy ground sausage. You can use pork or turkey sausage, but remember to choose something with a nice amount of fat. Do not use the lean dry stuff!

MAKES 24 TO 28 INDIVIDUAL PIES

For the dough:
5½ cups self-rising flour, plus
    more for dusting
1 teaspoon kosher salt
⅔ cup shortening
1½ cups whole milk
2 large eggs, lightly beaten

For the chimichurri:
1 bunch fresh cilantro
6 green onions, ends trimmed
1 small jalapeño, stem trimmed
1 teaspoon Creole seasoning
1 teaspoon minced fresh garlic
Juice of 1 large lime
1 cup extra-virgin olive oil

For the filling:
1½ pounds 80/20 ground beef
1½ pounds spicy ground pork or
    turkey sausage
1 large red onion, diced
2 tablespoons garlic powder
2½ teaspoons Creole seasoning
1 teaspoon seasoning salt
1 teaspoon ground black pepper
¼ cup all-purpose flour

Vegetable oil, for deep-frying

- To make the dough, in a large mixing bowl, combine the self-rising flour with the kosher salt. Whisk until combined. Next, add the shortening, milk, and eggs. Mix with a large fork until it forms into a ball of dough. Refrigerate the dough for at least 1 hour.

- While the dough chills, make the chimichurri. Place all ingredients in a food processor and pulse to the desired consistency. Transfer to a medium bowl and set aside.

- To make the filling, heat a large skillet over medium heat, add the beef and sausage, and cook, breaking up the meat, until browned all over. Pour off the excess fat. Toss in the onion, garlic powder, Creole seasoning, seasoning salt, and pepper. Cook, stirring occasionally, until the onions are softened, about 5 minutes. Sprinkle in the all-purpose flour and stir until well incorporated. Remove the skillet from the heat and let the filling cool.

- Next, roll out the dough on a lightly floured surface until ⅛ inch thick. Cut into about two dozen 5-inch rounds.

- Spoon some of the filling onto one half of each round, then fold the other dough half over it. Use a fork to crimp the edges closed.

- Pour enough oil into a deep fryer or deep skillet to deep-fry the pies, and heat it to 360 to 375 degrees F. Fry the pies until they are nice and evenly golden brown, 5 to 8 minutes, flipping them as needed.

- Remove the pies from the oil and place them on a paper-towel-lined plate to absorb the excess oil. Serve with the chimichurri on the side for dipping.

Breakin' Bread

Hot-Water Cornbread	86
Cracklin' Cornbread	88
Savory Monkey Bread	91
Three-Cheese, Bacon, and Herb Biscuits	92
Garlicky Cheese Drop Biscuits	94
Red Velvet Biscuits	95
Cherry Pie Biscuits	96
Butter Pecan Scones	99
Hummingbird Bread	100
Apple Fritter Bread	101
Real Deal Beignets	104

Hot-Water Cornbread

FAN FAVE!

My family loves all types of cornbread, especially sweet cornbread in loaves. But if you don't want to crank up the oven, hot water cornbread is the way to go. We love it with fish fries because you can just drop the patties into the oil when frying fish. This style of cornbread also pairs well with Southern beans, greens, and cabbage. Feel free to serve some sweet tea to go with your meal!

MAKES 8 SERVINGS	
¾ cup vegetable oil	2 tablespoons sugar
1½ cups yellow cornmeal	1½ cups boiling water
½ cup self-rising flour	

◆ Pour the vegetable oil into a medium skillet (I use my cast iron) and heat over medium heat.

◆ Meanwhile, combine the cornmeal, flour, and sugar in a medium mixing bowl. Sift or whisk until everything is well combined. Next, pour in the hot water a little at a time, whisking after each addition, until a dough forms. Form the dough into about 8 patties, each about 3 inches.

◆ Working in batches so you don't overcrowd the skillet, fry the patties in the oil until golden, 1 to 2 minutes on each side. Remove the cornbread from the oil, and place on a paper-towel-lined plate to drain. Cool slightly before serving.

Cracklin' Cornbread

I didn't like cracklings as a kid, but something changed when I was twelve and I came around! I decided to try baking cracklings into a savory cornbread because why the heck not? Some people use bacon and some use pork trimmings from a roast. Both of those methods are good (although I personally find bacon too salty), but I like to add crispy pork belly. I also add herbs, which isn't as common, but the garlic and thyme give it a nice flavor. And I love the spice of the red pepper flakes, but just skip that if spicy isn't your thing. Serve it as a side, especially with Soulful Cabbage and Collard Greens (page 164). Or crumble it over beans and you have a winner.

MAKES ONE 9-BY-13-INCH CORNBREAD

For the cracklings:
2 cups vegetable oil
½ pound fatty pork belly with skin, cut into small cubes
1 teaspoon garlic powder
1 teaspoon onion powder

For the cornbread:
6 tablespoons melted butter, plus more for greasing

3 cups all-purpose flour
1½ cups yellow cornmeal
2 tablespoons baking powder
1 teaspoon kosher salt
6 large eggs, lightly beaten
2½ cups whole milk
⅔ cup vegetable oil
2 teaspoons minced garlic
1 teaspoon dried thyme
1 teaspoon red pepper flakes

- First, make the cracklings. Heat the 2 cups vegetable oil in a large deep skillet to 300 degrees F.

- Meanwhile, sprinkle the pork belly with the garlic powder and onion powder.

- Working in batches to avoid overcrowding the skillet, fry the pork belly until golden brown, 15 to 20 minutes. Remove the pork from the skillet and let it drain and cool on a paper-towel-lined plate.

- While the pork cools, increase the oil temperature to 375 degrees F.

- Carefully add the pork back into the skillet and cook until the skin is nice and crisp, about 10 minutes. Remove the pork from the skillet, and let cool again on a fresh stack of paper towels.

- Preheat the oven to 350 degrees F. Butter a 9-by-13-inch baking dish.

- To make the cornbread, in a large bowl, sift or whisk together the flour, cornmeal, baking powder, and salt. Next, add the eggs, milk, ⅔ cup vegetable oil, and melted butter. Whisk until well combined. Add the cracklings, garlic, thyme, and red pepper flakes and fold them into the batter.

- Pour the batter into the prepared baking dish. Bake for 25 to 30 minutes, or until a toothpick inserted into the center comes out clean. Let cool for 5 to 10 minutes before serving.

Savory Monkey Bread

I hope we've all had a tasty pull-apart monkey bread with brown sugar and cinnamon. I thought it would be different and delicious to try a savory version. Cheese and bacon and green onions really make this bread special. The cheese crisps up on the edges and bacon is both crunchy and chewy.

This bread is simple but feels like such a treat. I like to serve it on Christmas, Mother's Day, and Easter. It's a great choice for brunch, but these biscuits will dress up any meal. Try it with fried pork chops and my favorite braised cabbage (page 164).

MAKES 12 SERVINGS

Nonstick cooking spray
2 (16-ounce) cans large biscuits
 (8 biscuits per can)
½ cup cooked crumbled
 breakfast sausage
½ cup cooked crumbled
 smoked bacon
1½ cups shredded pepper jack cheese
½ cup diced red bell pepper
¼ cup chopped green onions

◆ Preheat the oven to 350 degrees F. Spray a Bundt pan with nonstick cooking spray.

◆ Open the cans of biscuits, and cut each biscuit into fours. Toss them into a large bowl along with the sausage, bacon, cheese, bell pepper, and green onions. Transfer everything to the prepared Bundt pan and let sit for 10 minutes.

◆ Bake for 15 to 20 minutes, or until the monkey bread is golden brown. Remove from the oven and let cool slightly. Serve warm and enjoy.

Three-Cheese, Bacon, and Herb Biscuits

Everybody likes the Cheddar Bay Biscuits from Red Lobster, but I always found them very salty. So I decided to put my own spin on them. In this recipe you really get that wonderful fresh biscuit flavor without all the salt, and the cheese and bacon really come through to give you a tastier biscuit in my opinion.

In addition to cheddar, I use Colby Jack and smoked Gouda. The bacon adds this savory, smoky flavor that makes these biscuits perfect with seafood; for breakfast with eggs, grits, or ham; or just on their own.

MAKES 12 SMALL BISCUITS

Butter or shortening, for greasing
8 slices bacon
2 cups all-purpose flour
1 tablespoon baking powder
2 teaspoons herbes de Provence
1 teaspoon onion powder
1 teaspoon garlic powder
½ teaspoon kosher salt
½ cup (1 stick) frozen unsalted butter, shredded on a cheese grater

1 cup buttermilk
½ cup shredded sharp cheddar cheese
½ cup shredded Colby Jack cheese
½ cup shredded or crumbled smoked Gouda
3 tablespoons salted butter, melted, for brushing
1 tablespoon chopped fresh parsley, for garnish

◆ Preheat the oven to 425 degrees F. Lightly grease a baking sheet.

◆ Place a large skillet over medium heat, then add the bacon and cook, flipping once, until it's nice and crisp, about 5 minutes. Remove the bacon from the skillet and set aside to cool, but reserve 1 tablespoon of the rendered fat. Crumble or chop the bacon.

◆ In a large bowl, whisk together the flour, baking powder, herbes de Provence, onion powder, garlic powder, and salt. Next, add the shredded butter and pour in the buttermilk, and work them into the dough. Gently fold in all three cheeses, the crumbled bacon, and the reserved 1 tablespoon bacon fat.

◆ Use a ¼-cup measuring cup to scoop the dough onto the prepared baking sheet. Bake the biscuits for 12 to 15 minutes, or until they are fluffy and risen.

◆ Remove the pan from the oven. Brush the biscuits with the melted butter and sprinkle with the parsley. Serve warm.

Garlicky Cheese Drop Biscuits

These are a simple and straightforward side for fried fish. Just scoop the batter with an ice cream scoop or tablespoon and drop it right onto a baking sheet! The texture is flaky on the outside, very soft and almost gooey in the middle. They're best when served fresh out of the oven. I like the spicy peppers in the pepper jack and also love that the white cheese doesn't turn the biscuits orange. I'm funny that way! Regardless of the color, the result is a delicate, flavorful little biscuit.

MAKES 12 BISCUITS

Nonstick baking spray
2 cups all-purpose flour
1 tablespoon sugar
1 tablespoon baking powder
1 teaspoon garlic powder
1 teaspoon kosher salt

1 cup half-and-half
¾ cup (1½ sticks) unsalted butter, melted, divided
1½ cups shredded pepper jack cheese
1 tablespoon minced garlic
½ teaspoon dried parsley flakes

◆ Preheat the oven to 425 degrees F. Spray a baking sheet with baking spray.

◆ In a large mixing bowl, whisk or sift together the flour, sugar, baking powder, garlic powder, and salt. Pour in the half-and-half and ½ cup of the butter. Mix the ingredients until well combined. Next, fold in the cheese and minced garlic.

◆ Scoop out the dough onto the prepared baking sheet, leaving 2 to 3 inches between each biscuit. (Each scoop should be 2 to 3 tablespoons.) Bake for 10 to 15 minutes, or until the biscuits are golden brown.

◆ In a small bowl, combine the parsley with the remaining ¼ cup butter and mix well. Brush onto the warm biscuits. Serve and enjoy!

Red Velvet Biscuits

FAN FAVE!

I invented these biscuits to keep up with my friend Denise for a Christmas brunch video. She always creates fabulous tablescapes with over-the-top decor. I knew I couldn't just show up with some plain ol' biscuits, so this recipe was born. These are sweeter than your average biscuits but not overly so. Like with most red velvet recipes, I use vanilla extract and unsweetened cocoa powder here. You will taste a hint of both, but it isn't overwhelming. I also use a combo of butter and butter-flavored shortening—the butter makes the biscuits soft and flavorful, while the shortening makes them nice and flaky. Make Valentine's Day, Mother's Day, or Easter extra special with these fun, festive biscuits. I even love them with fried chicken.

MAKES ABOUT 10 BISCUITS

¼ cup (½ stick) unsalted butter, softened, for greasing, brushing, and serving

2 cups self-rising flour, plus more for dusting

2 tablespoons sugar

1 tablespoon unsweetened cocoa powder

½ teaspoon cream of tartar

⅛ teaspoon kosher salt

¾ cup cold buttermilk

½ cup (1 stick) cold unsalted butter, shredded on a cheese grater

¼ cup butter-flavored vegetable shortening

1 teaspoon vanilla extract

Red food coloring

Honey, for serving

◆ Preheat the oven to 400 degrees F. Lightly grease a 9-by-13-inch baking dish with butter.

◆ In the bowl of a stand mixer with the dough hook attachment, combine the flour, sugar, cocoa powder, cream of tartar, and salt. Whisk until well combined. Add the buttermilk, shredded butter, shortening, vanilla, and a few drops of the food coloring until the desired color is reached (I use 8 drops). Mix on medium speed until a red dough forms, about 2 minutes.

◆ Lightly flour a work surface and rolling pin. Roll the dough to ½ inch thick, then fold it into quarters to create the biscuit layers. Flatten the dough once more to about ½ inch thick. Cut out the biscuits using a small canning jar lid, biscuit cutter, or cookie cutter.

◆ Transfer the biscuits to the prepared baking dish. Bake for 12 to 15 minutes, or until the biscuits are fluffy and risen.

◆ Brush or rub softened butter on top of the biscuits while they are still warm. Serve with more softened butter and honey.

Cherry Pie Biscuits

I once had a craving for apple pie biscuits but didn't have apples on hand. So I substituted canned cherries, which was pretty darn good. But I wanted to try it with fresh or frozen cherries and that's when it really came together. The pastry is flaky but the cherry juices make it soft, and the result is a delicious tender biscuit.

I serve these in the morning instead of pancakes or waffles. Or try them alongside eggs, bacon, and sausage. For dessert, they are great topped with vanilla ice cream.

MAKES 8 BISCUITS

For the biscuits:
Vegetable oil, for greasing
2 cups self-rising flour, plus
    more for dusting
4 tablespoons granulated
    sugar, divided
1½ teaspoons baking powder
1 teaspoon cream of tartar
⅛ teaspoon kosher salt
1¾ cups buttermilk
⅓ cup butter-flavored shortening

½ cup frozen cherries,
    thawed and minced
1 teaspoon almond extract
½ teaspoon ground cinnamon
¼ teaspoon ground nutmeg

For the icing:
1 cup powdered sugar
3 tablespoons half-and-half
1½ teaspoons almond extract

◆ Preheat the oven to 350 degrees F. Grease and flour a baking sheet.

◆ In a large mixing bowl, sift or whisk together the flour, 2 tablespoons of the granulated sugar, baking powder, cream of tartar, and salt. Next, add the buttermilk and shortening. Combine everything with a pastry cutter or fork until a dough forms.

◆ In a separate bowl, combine the minced cherries, almond extract, cinnamon, nutmeg, and remaining 2 tablespoons granulated sugar. Stir until well combined. Add to the biscuit dough, and work it in using your hands.

◆ Transfer the dough to a lightly floured surface and flatten the dough into a rectangle about 2 inches thick. Cut into 8 sections and place them on the prepared baking sheet.

◆ Bake for 10 to 15 minutes, or until the biscuits are golden brown. Remove from the oven and let the biscuits cool slightly.

◆ Meanwhile, in a medium bowl, combine the powdered sugar, half-and-half, and almond extract. Whisk until well combined, then drizzle over the warm biscuits. Serve and enjoy!

Butter Pecan Scones

My very favorite ice cream flavor is butter pecan. My mom made scones and biscuits all the time. You know I love to try new things in the kitchen, so I thought why not be creative and turn my favorite ice cream flavor into a scone? The result is pretty incredible. I like to serve these in the morning with coffee. The texture is a combination of biscuit and coffee cake, flaky, moist, and sweet. You will love these!

MAKES 6 SCONES

For the scones:
½ cup (1 stick) unsalted butter, plus more for greasing
¼ cup chopped pecans
2½ cups all-purpose flour, plus more for dusting
1 tablespoon baking powder
½ teaspoon kosher salt
¼ teaspoon baking soda

½ cup buttermilk
1 large egg, lightly beaten
½ cup dark brown sugar
2½ teaspoons vanilla extract

For the icing:
½ cup powdered sugar
2 teaspoons whole milk
1 teaspoon vanilla extract

- Preheat the oven to 400 degrees F. Lightly butter and flour a baking sheet.

- Melt the butter in a large skillet over medium heat. Add the pecans and cook for 2 minutes, until toasted. Remove the skillet from the heat and set aside to cool.

- In a large mixing bowl, sift or whisk together the flour, baking powder, salt, and baking soda.

- In a medium bowl, whisk together the buttermilk, egg, brown sugar, and vanilla extract. Using a spatula, scrape in the pecans and butter and stir to combine. Add the wet ingredients to the dry ingredients and stir just until blended—don't overmix.

- Transfer the dough to the prepared baking sheet and flatten it into a disk about ¾ inch thick. Cut into 6 equal wedges but don't pull them apart.

- Bake for about 20 minutes, or until the scones are light golden brown. Let cool for about 10 minutes, then carefully separate the scones.

- Meanwhile, whisk together the ingredients for the icing, then drizzle it over the warm scones. Serve with coffee or tea.

Hummingbird Bread

This is a take on hummingbird cake. I love cake in the morning, so I make a bread. That way I can feel okay about it, telling myself it's better for me than cake. Serve it cold, or toast it and spread with butter. Hummingbird cake is similar to carrot cake without the carrot—instead, it is a spiced cake with banana, pineapple, and coconut. It's not as sweet as cake because I don't put frosting on it. You don't need it; it's dense and moist as is.

MAKES 1 STANDARD LOAF PAN

¼ cup (½ stick) unsalted butter, softened, plus more for greasing
2½ cups all-purpose flour
1 teaspoon baking powder
½ teaspoon kosher salt
1 cup sugar
3 large eggs
¾ cup whole milk

2 teaspoons vanilla extract
2 medium bananas, chopped into small pieces
¼ cup crushed pineapple, drained
¼ cup sweetened coconut flakes
¾ teaspoon ground cinnamon
¼ teaspoon ground nutmeg

- Preheat the oven to 350 degrees F. Grease a standard loaf pan with butter.

- In a medium mixing bowl, stir together the flour, baking powder, and salt, then set aside.

- In a large mixing bowl, using a handheld mixer, cream the butter and sugar together. Slowly add the eggs, one at a time, and mix on medium speed after each addition until the batter is nice and creamy.

- Next, alternate adding the flour mixture with a little of the milk and mix until both are fully incorporated. Add the vanilla and stir. Fold in the bananas, pineapple, and coconut until well combined.

- Pour the batter into the prepared loaf pan and bake for 45 minutes to 1 hour, or until a toothpick inserted into the center comes out clean. Remove from the oven and let cool. Slice and enjoy!

Apple Fritter Bread

This loaf gives you all the flavor of an apple fritter donut without the deep-fried greasiness. You can certainly have it for dessert, but it's also a not-too-sweet slice that you can have with coffee or tea for breakfast. The key is using Granny Smith apples, which are tart enough to balance the sweetness. They also hold up really well when cooked, which makes them my favorite apples for baking.

MAKES 1 STANDARD LOAF PAN

For the bread:
½ cup unsalted butter, softened, plus more for greasing
2 cups all-purpose flour, plus more for dusting
¼ cup light brown sugar
2 teaspoons ground cinnamon, divided
½ teaspoon ground nutmeg
1½ cups granulated sugar, divided

3 medium Granny Smith apples, peeled, cored, and chopped
1¾ teaspoons baking powder
1 teaspoon kosher salt
2 large eggs
2 teaspoons vanilla extract
½ cup buttermilk

For the glaze:
1 cup powdered sugar
2 to 3 tablespoons half-and-half

- Preheat the oven to 350 degrees F. Lightly grease and flour a standard loaf pan.

- In a small bowl, combine the brown sugar with 1 teaspoon of the cinnamon and the nutmeg. Set to the side.

- In another small bowl, combine 1 tablespoon of the granulated sugar with the remaining 1 teaspoon cinnamon. Place the apples in a medium mixing bowl, then sprinkle them with the cinnamon-sugar. Toss the apples until they are well coated, then set to the side.

- In a separate mixing bowl, whisk together the flour, baking powder, and salt.

- In a large mixing bowl, using a handheld mixer, cream together the eggs, butter, vanilla, and remaining granulated sugar. Alternate adding the flour mixture and the buttermilk to the egg mixture, mixing after each addition.

CONTINUED

- Add half of the batter to the prepared loaf pan. Top with half of the apples, followed by half of the brown sugar mixture. Repeat with the remaining batter, apples, and brown sugar mixture.

- Bake for about 1 hour, or until a toothpick inserted into the center of the loaf comes out with a few moist crumbs. Remove from the oven and let cool for 10 minutes before removing from the pan.

- While the bread cools, make the glaze. In a small bowl, whisk the powdered sugar with 2 tablespoons of the half-and-half until well combined. Add 1 more tablespoon of half-and-half if you want a thinner glaze.

- Spoon the glaze all over the apple fritter bread, and let sit for about 15 minutes before serving.

Real Deal Beignets

We had beignets often when I was growing up so I like them "real"—not the fake stuff that just tastes like sugared biscuits at, ahem, certain fast food places. Calling those beignets is disrespectful, and personally it really burns my biscuits! This recipe isn't a shortcut, but it is easy to follow. I tried to make my version as simple as possible because people can get lost in the sauce. The texture should be almost like the elephant ears you get at fairs, a little crisp outside while light and fluffy inside. A proper beignet should not taste like a biscuit under any circumstance!

MAKES 24 BEIGNETS

¾ cup warm water

1 (0.25–ounce) packet active
   dry yeast

⅓ cup plus 2 teaspoons granulated
   sugar, divided

½ cup half-and-half

1 large egg, lightly beaten

3 tablespoons unsalted
   butter, softened

2 teaspoons vanilla extract

¼ teaspoon kosher salt

4 cups all-purpose flour, plus more
   for dusting

Vegetable oil, for greasing and frying

¼ cup powdered sugar

♦ In a small mixing bowl, combine the warm water with the yeast and 2 teaspoons of the sugar. Stir until the sugar dissolves. Let sit until the yeast foams, about 5 minutes.

♦ In a separate large mixing bowl, add the half-and-half, egg, butter, vanilla, salt, and remaining ⅓ cup sugar. Add the yeast mixture and stir. Gradually add the flour, and mix using a handheld or stand mixer with the dough hook attachment on medium speed (or with your hands) until a ball of dough forms.

♦ Transfer the dough to a lightly floured surface and knead for about 4 minutes, then place the dough in a lightly greased large bowl. Cover the bowl with a clean kitchen towel, and let rest in a draft-free area until the dough doubles in size, about 2 hours.

♦ Punch the dough to release the air, then knead on a lightly floured surface for 2 minutes. Roll out the dough until ½ inch thick, then cut it into 24 (3–inch) squares. You can cut them bigger or smaller as desired. Let the dough rest for 10 to 15 minutes before frying.

* Pour 1½ inches of vegetable oil into a large deep pan over medium-high heat. Heat the oil to about 360 degrees F.

* Working in batches, fry the beignets, flipping once, until they are golden brown, about 2 minutes. Remove the beignets from the oil, and place on a paper-towel-lined plate to drain.

* Dust with the powdered sugar and serve immediately.

The Halves and Have Hots

Not Yo' Mama's Bacon Caesar Salad   108

Cousin Rosie's Macaroni Salad   110

Mardi Gras Pasta Salad   111

Cajun Chicken Pasta Salad   113

Fried Tilapia Sandwiches   114

Muffuletta   117

Spicy Catfish and Oyster Po'boys   118

Country Steak Chili   120

Not Yo' Mama's Bacon Caesar Salad

I recall having Caesar salad when I visited people's houses growing up. It was the regular schmegular kind made with bottled dressing, and I was never a big fan. Then I tried the absolute best Caesar salad at the Golden Steer Steakhouse in Las Vegas. They make it tableside with a lot of ingredients. So many that I could never remember them all. This recipe is my attempt at recreating that dish at home. It's the only Caesar salad I like if I can't make it to Vegas. My go-to order at the Golden Steer is salmon, so pair this salad with my Blackened Salmon (page 127).

MAKES 6 TO 8 SERVINGS

For the dressing:
1 cup mayonnaise
1 cup sour cream
¼ cup red wine vinegar
3 garlic cloves, minced
2 tablespoons grated
    Parmesan cheese
2 teaspoons extra-virgin olive oil
2 teaspoons Worcestershire sauce
1 teaspoon freshly squeezed
    lemon juice

1 teaspoon anchovy paste
1 teaspoon Tabasco or your choice of
    hot sauce
1 teaspoon coarse black pepper
¼ teaspoon red pepper flakes

For the salad:
½ pound thick-cut hickory bacon
8½ cups chopped romaine hearts
½ cup shredded Parmesan cheese
1 cup garlic Parmesan croutons

◆ To make the dressing, in a large mixing bowl, combine the mayonnaise and sour cream and stir until well combined. Add the remaining dressing ingredients and stir until nice and creamy. Pour the dressing into a jar or bowl, then set to the side.

◆ To make the salad, first place a large skillet over medium heat, then add the bacon and cook, flipping once, until it's nice and crisp, 7 to 8 minutes. Remove the bacon from the skillet and let cool on a paper-towel-lined plate. Crumble or chop the bacon.

◆ In a large bowl, combine the romaine, shredded Parmesan, croutons, and bacon. Add the desired amount of dressing and toss until the salad is nicely coated. Refrigerate the remaining dressing for up to 7 days, or serve on the side. Enjoy!

Cousin Rosie's Macaroni Salad

FAN FAVE!

Although this macaroni salad is not entirely "classic," it's as close to classic as I'm going to get. The base is the familiar macaroni with green and red bell peppers in a sweet-tangy creamy dressing. But I load it up with hard-boiled eggs. As simple as it is, this is one of my most requested dishes for cookouts and picnics. The macaroni salad benefits from chilling in the fridge, so it's worth making in advance to let the flavors marry.

MAKES 8 SERVINGS

Kosher salt, for boiling the pasta

2 cups macaroni pasta

1 cup mayonnaise

2 tablespoons sweet relish or dill relish (depending on your preference)

1 tablespoon distilled white vinegar

3 hard-boiled eggs, cooled and diced

¼ cup diced carrots

¼ cup chopped green onions

¼ cup diced green bell pepper

¼ cup diced red bell pepper

1 tablespoon seasoning salt

1 teaspoon coarse black pepper

½ teaspoon sugar

- Bring a large pot of salted water to a boil over high heat. Cook the pasta until it is al dente (cooked but still firm), then drain the pasta and set aside to cool.

- In a large mixing bowl, stir together the mayonnaise, relish, and vinegar until combined. Add the rest of the ingredients, including the pasta, and gently fold everything together until well incorporated.

- Transfer the salad to a large storage bowl and cover. Place in the refrigerator until chilled, at least 1 hour, before serving.

Mardi Gras Pasta Salad

Come Mardi Gras time, this is a dish I make a lot. It has crawfish, lobster, cilantro, and Creole seasoning, along with the holy trinity of onions, celery, and bell peppers. It's festive and let me tell you, it's a lot easier than making gumbo! You can bring this dish to potlucks or cookouts, and everyone always loves it! I usually use tricolor rotini, but cavatappi is another great shape for the pasta. To make it even more celebratory, serve it on a platter with Mardi Gras colors.

MAKES 12 SERVINGS

Kosher salt, for boiling the pasta
6½ cups tricolor rotini pasta
1¾ cups mayonnaise
2 tablespoons freshly squeezed lemon juice
2 pounds cooked lobster meat, chilled and chopped
2 pounds cooked crawfish meat, chilled and chopped

1 medium red bell pepper, diced
3 stalks celery, diced
1 medium red onion, diced
5 green onions, chopped
½ cup chopped fresh cilantro
3½ teaspoons Creole seasoning
2 teaspoons seafood seasoning
1½ teaspoons coarse black pepper

- Bring a large pot of salted water to a boil over high heat. Cook the pasta until it is al dente (cooked but still firm), then drain the pasta and set aside to cool.

- In a large mixing bowl, stir together the mayonnaise and lemon juice until well incorporated. Next, add the lobster, crawfish, bell pepper, celery, red and green onions, and cilantro. Sprinkle in the Creole and seafood seasonings and black pepper, then toss everything together. Finally, fold in the pasta until well incorporated.

- Transfer the salad to a large storage bowl and cover. Place in the refrigerator until chilled, at least 2 hours. Taste and add more seasoning to your liking. Serve and enjoy!

Cajun Chicken Pasta Salad

Here's a chicken pasta salad that I jazzed up with some Cajun flavor. This isn't your everyday boring pasta salad. It's packed with chicken, bell pepper, red onions, and a creamy mayo-based dressing. This pasta salad should be chilled before serving. It makes the perfect side dish for summer barbecues or office potlucks.

MAKES 10 SERVINGS

Kosher salt, for boiling the pasta

6½ cups small pasta shells

1¾ cups mayonnaise

1 tablespoon light brown sugar

2 teaspoons freshly squeezed lemon juice

1 (4–pound) rotisserie chicken, skin and bones removed, meat chopped

2 large slicing tomatoes (such as beefsteak), diced

1 medium red bell pepper, diced

1 medium red onion, diced

5 green onions, chopped

1 bunch fresh parsley, chopped

1 tablespoon Cajun seasoning

1½ teaspoons coarse black pepper

Dried parsley flakes and paprika, for sprinkling (optional)

- Bring a large pot of salted water to a boil over high heat. Cook the pasta until it is al dente (cooked but still firm), then drain the pasta and set aside to cool.

- In a large mixing bowl, stir together the mayonnaise, brown sugar, and lemon juice until well incorporated. Next, add the chicken, tomatoes, bell pepper, red and green onions, and fresh parsley. Fold everything together. Then add the pasta, sprinkle in the Cajun seasoning and black pepper, and fold again until well combined.

- Transfer the salad to a large storage bowl and cover. Place in the refrigerator until chilled, at least 2 hours.

- Remove from the refrigerator, and sprinkle parsley flakes and paprika on top, if desired. Serve and enjoy!

Fried Tilapia Sandwiches

I love a good fried fish sandwich, but lot of restaurants don't serve them anymore. When they do, they don't measure up: too much batter with a cold slice of cheese. A cold slice of cheese just feels lazy! I don't like lazy but I do like simple, and fried fish sandwiches come together easily at home. You can use white or yellow cornmeal—whatever you have on hand.

My fish sandwich is straightforward: I want to taste the fish—no cheese please—a little tartar sauce, and great bread. I don't like a thick batter; who wants bread on bread? I like mine with a thin cornmeal coating. This way the fish inside cooks perfectly but the outside stays crispy.

MAKES 6 SANDWICHES

1 cup white or yellow cornmeal	3 teaspoons yellow mustard
¼ cup all-purpose flour	1½ cups vegetable oil
3 teaspoons seafood seasoning	Spicy tartar sauce (see page 118)
1 teaspoon onion powder	12 slices white bread
1 teaspoon garlic powder	1 cup shredded lettuce
6 (6-ounce) tilapia fillets	Hot sauce, for serving

♦ Combine the cornmeal, flour, seafood seasoning, onion powder, and garlic powder in a plastic bag. Shake everything until well mixed.

♦ Coat the tilapia with the mustard, then place the pieces, one at a time, into the plastic bag. Shake the bag, making sure the fillet is nicely coated, then remove and set on a plate. Repeat with the remaining pieces.

♦ In a large skillet, heat the vegetable oil over medium-high heat until it reaches about 360 degrees F. Carefully place the fillets, one at a time, in the oil and fry, flipping once, until the breading is golden brown and the fish is cooked through, 5 to 7 minutes per side. Remove the fish from the oil and place on a paper-towel-lined plate to absorb the excess oil. Repeat with the remaining fillets.

♦ Spread spicy tartar on each slice of bread, add lettuce to the 6 bottom slices, and top with the fish. Cover with the top slices. Serve with hot sauce.

Muffuletta

I love all dishes that use olives in special ways! Olives give anything a salty, briny, creamy mild bite. The Muffuletta sandwich is such a popular Mardi Gras recipe that it made sense to include it in this book. Mine is traditional but I use less meat so you can taste all the toppings and the delicious bread. Of course I did sneak red pepper flakes into my recipe because I can't help but love that heat! I do recommend letting the sandwich hang out in the fridge for a few hours. You really want the olive salad flavors to marry—it comes through so much better! Aside from Mardi Gras, you can serve this on football Sundays. Cut the sandwich into small pieces and add fancy toothpicks. Double or triple this recipe depending on how many sandwiches you need.

MAKES ONE 12-INCH SANDWICH (4 SERVINGS)

For the olive salad:
¼ cup pitted green olives, minced
¼ cup pitted black olives, minced
¼ small red bell pepper, minced
3 large peperoncini, minced
3 tablespoons diced red onion
3 garlic cloves, minced
2 teaspoons extra-virgin olive oil
2 teaspoons red wine vinegar
1 teaspoon dried basil
½ teaspoon red pepper flakes

For the sandwich:
1 (12-inch-long) loaf Italian bread,
    split lengthwise
½ pound ham, thinly sliced
¼ pound salami
¼ pound capicola
¼ pound provolone cheese,
    thinly sliced

◆ In a medium mixing bowl, combine all the olive salad ingredients and stir until well combined. Spread a nice thick layer of olive salad on the bottom half of the bread.

◆ Next, layer the meats and cheese on top of the olive salad, then top with the remaining olive salad.

◆ Cover with the top half of the bread, then wrap the sandwich with butcher paper. Refrigerate for 3 hours before slicing and serving.

Spicy Catfish and Oyster Po'boys

Years ago, I did a collab with YouTuber Diane DiMeo, and she made a po'boy with oysters. I thought it was really clever. I liked the oysters combined with spicy catfish and decided to make it into a po'boy. I use hoagie rolls, and I know I might lose some points with my cousins down South but I am a Northerner. You could certainly use French bread instead if you're a purist. I use oysters that are already shucked in a jar that I find in the seafood aisle, so you don't have to worry about shucking them yourself.

MAKES 4 SANDWICHES

For the spicy tartar:
¼ cup mayonnaise
2 tablespoons yellow mustard
1 tablespoon dill relish
2 teaspoons freshly squeezed
   lemon juice
1 teaspoon minced red onion
½ teaspoon red pepper flakes

For the po'boys:
1 cup self-rising flour
½ cup yellow cornmeal

2 teaspoons Creole seasoning
1 teaspoon cayenne pepper
1 pound catfish fillets, cut into 2-inch
   pieces
1 pound jarred or freshly shucked
   medium oysters, drained
¼ cup yellow mustard
2 to 2½ cups vegetable oil, for frying
4 French bread hoagie rolls
1 cup shredded lettuce

• To make the spicy tartar, in a small bowl, stir together the mayonnaise, mustard, relish, lemon juice, red onion, and red pepper flakes until well combined. Cover and refrigerate the spicy tartar until ready to use.

• To make the po'boys, first, in a large bowl, combine the flour, cornmeal, Creole seasoning, and cayenne and mix well.

• Coat the catfish and oysters with the mustard, then dip them into the flour mixture until coated on all sides. Transfer to a plate and let sit for about 5 minutes so the coating will stick.

- Meanwhile, heat the vegetable oil in a large deep skillet or deep fryer until it reaches 350 to 375 degrees F.

- Working in batches to avoid overcrowding, carefully fry the catfish until golden brown, about 8 minutes. Remove from the oil and set on a paper-towel-lined plate or baking sheet. Next, fry the oysters until golden brown, then transfer them to the paper-towel-lined plate to drain.

- Finally, stuff the hoagies with the oysters and catfish. Sprinkle lettuce on top, then drizzle with spicy tartar. Enjoy!

Country Steak Chili

One of my relatives from the country always made her chili with chopped steak, so I started calling this version "country." The steak gives the chili a different taste and texture than the usual ground beef. I love this version so much that now when my husband buys a cut of steak I don't like, I turn it into chili. It's a great way to use tougher cuts of meat (like sirloin steak) that benefit from a longer simmering time to bring out their tenderness. I also add a good amount of fresh cilantro because I love the taste, but feel free to leave it out if you're not a fan.

MAKES 6 TO 8 SERVINGS

For the chili:
2 tablespoons vegetable oil
3 pounds sirloin steak, cubed
1 large red onion, diced
1 red bell pepper, diced
1 green bell pepper, diced
4 cups beef broth
8 ounces tomato paste
1 tablespoon Worcestershire sauce
2 (14.5-ounce) cans fire-roasted
    tomatoes
1 (14.5-ounce) can kidney beans, rinsed
    and drained
2 cups frozen corn

½ bunch cilantro, chopped
3 to 4 garlic cloves, minced
1 (1.25-ounce) packet chili seasoning mix
1 tablespoon seasoning salt
1½ teaspoons ground black pepper
3 dashes Tabasco

For serving (all toppings optional):
Your choice of shredded cheese
Lime wedges
Jalapeño slices
Diced onion
Sour cream
Red pepper flakes

* Heat the oil in a large skillet over medium-high meat. Once it is nice and hot, toss in the steak and cook until browned, 4 to 5 minutes, then transfer to a plate. Next, add the onion and bell peppers and cook until soft, about 3 minutes, then remove the skillet from the heat.

* In a large pot over medium heat, combine the beef broth, tomato paste, and Worcestershire. Whisk until well combined. Stir in the steak, onion, and bell peppers, then add the tomatoes, kidney beans, corn, cilantro, garlic, chili mix, seasoning salt, black pepper, and Tabasco and stir well.

* Reduce the heat to medium-low and simmer the chili for about 2 hours, or until the beef is very tender. Ladle the chili into bowls and serve with your desired toppings.

Main Squeezes

Jamaican Jerk Shrimp and Peppers	124
Blackened Salmon	127
Seafood Lasagna	128
Seafood Boil with Creole Garlic Sauce	131
Butterflied Herb-Roasted Chicken	133
Bacon-Wrapped Stuffed Chicken Thighs	134
Best Damn Chicken and Dumplings	136
Easy Smoked Whole Turkey	139
Slow Cooker Smothered Turkey Wings	141
Deep-Fried Cornish Game Hens	145
Philly Cheesesteak Lasagna	147
Easy Slow Cooker Short Ribs	151
Jamaican Oxtails	152
Grilled Lamb Chops	155
Cajun-Style Leg of Lamb	156
Stuffed Pork Chops	157
Blackberry-Glazed Ribs	158
Slow Cooker Neck Bones and Potatoes	161

Jamaican Jerk Shrimp and Peppers

I love jerk chicken and jerk pork, so I thought why not jerk shrimp? The jerk seasoning preparation isn't usually associated with seafood but it really works. The spiciness is relatively mild so feel free to add red pepper flakes to bump up the heat level. This is a great recipe to have in your back pocket because it's easy and quick but still feels fancy.

MAKES 6 SERVINGS	
2 tablespoons salted butter, plus more for greasing	1 medium red bell pepper, thinly sliced
2 pounds jumbo shrimp, peeled and deveined, tails left on	4 garlic cloves, minced
3 tablespoons extra-virgin olive oil	2½ teaspoons jerk seasoning
1 medium green bell pepper, thinly sliced	1 teaspoon seafood seasoning
	1 teaspoon smoked paprika

◆ Preheat the oven to 375 degrees F. Butter a 9-by-13-inch baking dish, then add the shrimp and set to the side.

◆ In a large skillet over medium heat, add the olive oil and butter. Toss in the bell peppers and cook, stirring occasionally, until slightly softened, 3 to 4 minutes, then add the garlic. Pour over the shrimp.

◆ Sprinkle the shrimp with the jerk seasoning, seafood seasoning, and paprika and stir until well coated.

◆ Cover the baking dish with aluminum foil and bake for 7 minutes. Remove from the oven and let sit for 2 minutes. Serve with the rice dish of your choice.

Blackened Salmon

Some people see blackened fish and think it's burned, but that's a misconception. The blackened color comes from the seasonings, usually paprika and cayenne pepper, which darken as they cook. This blackened fish is a combo of my Louisiana roots and my upbringing in the Pacific Northwest. We have lots of salmon here, and as a Northwest girl, it's my go-to fish.

For my take, I add an unconventional ingredient: rosemary. I love the woodsy flavor with salmon. I was inspired by watching the movie *Boomerang*. Remember when Marcus cooked for Jacqueline? He mentioned that he used rosemary on his salmon, and I totally stole that idea and ended up loving it. Fun fact: Rosemary is not just one of my favorite herbs, it's my full name.

MAKES 4 SERVINGS

Nonstick cooking spray
1 pound salmon fillet, cut into fourths
1½ tablespoons salted butter, softened
2 teaspoons extra-virgin olive oil
1 teaspoon smoked paprika
1 teaspoon finely chopped
    fresh rosemary
1 teaspoon finely chopped fresh dill

1 teaspoon kosher salt
1 teaspoon onion powder
1 teaspoon garlic powder
½ teaspoon cayenne pepper
½ teaspoon ground thyme
Creamy Mashed Baby Reds (page 170),
    for serving

♦ Preheat the oven to 400 degrees F.

♦ Lightly spray a large baking dish with cooking spray, then place the salmon fillets inside.

♦ In a small bowl, combine the butter, olive oil, and all the herbs and seasonings. Whisk well, then brush onto the salmon fillets.

♦ Bake for 12 to 15 minutes, or until the salmon just flakes with a fork. During the last minute of baking, switch the oven to broil. Remove from the oven and serve with the mashed potatoes.

Seafood Lasagna

The first time I made seafood lasagna was on Facebook and my blog, and I did it as a collab with another YouTuber, Daym Drops. I couldn't think of what I wanted to make, and Daym suggested we think outside the box and use seafood. It turned out to be both delicious and different. People have seafood alfredo, so why not lasagna? This recipe was a game changer. You can use fresh crab or canned, whatever your pockets allow. If lobster is not available, substitute more crab. I make a cheesy white sauce, extra creamy from the Havarti. It is rich, I'm not gonna lie!

MAKES 8 TO 12 SERVINGS

Vegetable oil, for greasing

Kosher salt, for boiling the pasta

9 lasagna noodles

1 pound cooked lobster
    meat, chopped

1 pound cooked crabmeat, chopped

1 pound raw shrimp meat, diced

½ cup chopped green onions

4 teaspoons Old Bay Seasoning or
    your choice of seafood seasoning

5 tablespoons salted butter

3 tablespoons all-purpose flour

3 cups heavy cream

5 garlic cloves, minced

2 teaspoons seasoning salt

1 teaspoon coarse black pepper

1 cup shredded Parmesan

2 cups cubed creamy Havarti

1½ cups shredded mozzarella cheese

Dried parsley flakes, for sprinkling

◆ Preheat the oven to 350 degrees F. Lightly grease a 9-by-13-inch baking dish.

◆ Bring a large pot of salted water to a boil and cook the lasagna noodles according to the package directions, then drain.

◆ Meanwhile, in a large mixing bowl, toss the lobster, crab, and shrimp meats with the green onions, then sprinkle in the Old Bay. Fold the ingredients until well combined, then set to the side.

◆ Next, melt the butter in a large saucepan over medium heat. Sprinkle in the flour, and whisk until well combined. Pour in the heavy cream, then whisk until lump-free. Cook the sauce until it thickens, then sprinkle in the garlic, seasoning salt, and black pepper. Whisk well and add in the Parmesan. Whisk some more, then cook for 2 more minutes. Remove the saucepan from the heat.

- Combine the Havarti and mozzarella in a large bowl, then set to the side.

- Add a little of the cheese sauce to the bottom of the prepared baking dish. Next, lay down 3 of the lasagna noodles, followed by half of the seafood mixture. Top with one-third of the cheese sauce and one-third of the Havarti and mozzarella. Repeat with another layer in the same order. Finally, top the lasagna with the remaining 3 lasagna noodles, cheese sauce, and Havarti and mozzarella.

- Sprinkle some parsley flakes on top, then cover the lasagna with aluminum foil. Bake for 1 hour and 25 minutes. Remove from the oven and let sit for about 15 minutes before serving.

Seafood Boil with Creole Garlic Sauce

FAN FAVE!

This recipe will make sure that your seafood boil is on point! I don't want y'all out there using that bottled stuff for the seasoning either. I make a natural version with herbs and aromatics that tastes even better than the store-bought mix. And you can do it all on the kitchen stovetop if you don't have access to outdoor space.

Dipping the seafood in the Creole garlic sauce takes this seafood boil to a whole other level. I love serving this for Fourth of July gatherings and later in the summer when corn is in season. It's a luxurious sort of dish, packed with lobster tails and crab legs and claws, but it feels casual because everyone's eating with their hands. To go really big, use king crab instead of Dungeness.

MAKES 6 TO 8 SERVINGS

For the seafood boil:
2 large lemons, cut into wedges
1 medium yellow onion, sliced
6 to 8 garlic cloves, peeled
3 sprigs of fresh parsley
2 sprigs of fresh thyme
3 sprigs of fresh dill
½ cup (1 stick) salted butter
2 tablespoons Creole seasoning
1 tablespoon apple cider vinegar
2 pounds andouille sausage or your
   favorite smoked sausage, cut into
   large pieces
8 ears of corn, husks and silk removed,
   cobs cut into thirds
5 medium potatoes (I use russets), cut
   into large pieces

3 pounds Dungeness crab legs
1 pound Dungeness crab claws
4 to 6 (4-ounce) lobster tails
2 pounds jumbo shrimp, peeled and
   deveined, tails left on

For the sauce:
½ cup (1 stick) salted butter
Juice from 1 large lemon
3 tablespoons mild hot sauce
1½ tablespoons minced garlic
2 teaspoons paprika
2 teaspoons dried parsley flakes
1½ teaspoons Creole seasoning
½ teaspoon coarse black pepper

CONTINUED

◆ In a 24-quart pot over high heat, toss in the lemons, onion, garlic, and herbs. Add the butter, Creole seasoning, and vinegar. Pour in 16 cups water, bring to a boil, then turn the heat down to medium-high and simmer for 45 minutes. Reduce the heat to medium.

◆ Using a slotted spoon, fish out all (or as much as you can) of the solid ingredients from the pot and discard them.

◆ Add the sausage and corn. Stir, cover, and simmer for 15 minutes. Next, add the potatoes, and simmer, uncovered, for 10 minutes. Add the crab legs and claws and lobster tails. Simmer, uncovered, for 15 minutes.

◆ Finally, toss in the shrimp, stir, and remove the pot from the heat. Cover and let sit for 10 minutes.

◆ Meanwhile, in a small saucepan, combine all the sauce ingredients. Set over medium heat and cook until the butter is melted. Stir, reduce the heat to low, and continue cooking for 10 minutes.

◆ Transfer the seafood, sausage, corn, and potatoes to a large platter. You can pour the sauce over the seafood boil or serve it on the side in small bowls for dipping. Dig in!

Butterflied Herb-Roasted Chicken

When I was younger, I liked my chicken roasted more than fried. This recipe came about one day when I was playing with herbs I bought at the discount store. It turns out that a jar of herbes de Provence has a mix of herbs that's amazing with chicken (usually thyme, rosemary, tarragon, marjoram, lavender, and fennel).

I like to butterfly the chicken because I find that it cooks a tad bit quicker when I do so. The buttermilk tenderizes the bird and helps add a little saltiness to the meat.

MAKES 8 SERVINGS

1 (4- to 5-pound) whole chicken, cleaned (see Cleaning Poultry 101 on page 140) and butterflied (backbone removed, chicken spread out and flattened)
2 cups buttermilk
2 tablespoons extra-virgin olive oil
1 tablespoon herbes de Provence

2½ teaspoons seasoning salt
2 teaspoons garlic powder
2 teaspoons onion powder
1 teaspoon coarse black pepper
¼ teaspoon red pepper flakes
Corn Pudding Casserole (page 176), for serving

- Place the chicken in a brining bag and pour in the buttermilk. Seal the bag, then place in the refrigerator for 8 hours.

- Preheat the oven to 400 degrees F. Add 2 inches of water to a large roasting or baking pan, then set a rack in the pan. (The water prevents the chicken drippings from smoking!)

- Remove the chicken from the brining bag and transfer it to a baking sheet or cutting board. Discard the bag and buttermilk. Pat the chicken dry with a paper towel, then drizzle the olive oil all over the chicken.

- In a small bowl, combine the herbes de Provence, seasoning salt, garlic powder, onion powder, black pepper, and red pepper flakes and mix well. Sprinkle the seasoning all over the chicken, then massage it in.

- Place the chicken, breast side down, on the rack in the prepared roasting pan. Roast, uncovered, for 55 to 60 minutes, or until the internal temperature of the chicken reaches 165 degrees F. Remove from the oven, and let the chicken rest for 10 minutes before slicing. Serve with the corn pudding.

Bacon-Wrapped Stuffed Chicken Thighs

If you know me at all, you know I like bacon-wrapped anything. Plain chicken thighs are fine, but wrap them with smoky, salty bacon and they instantly grab my attention! Not only does the bacon get crisp on the chicken, it serves a practical purpose by keeping the stuffing from oozing out. The filling is a combo of frozen spinach, cream cheese, and pepper jack that becomes molten and creamy as it bakes.

MAKES 4 TO 6 SERVINGS

4 ounces cream cheese, at room temperature

3 tablespoons sour cream

½ pound pepper jack cheese, shredded

½ cup frozen spinach, thawed and squeezed to remove excess liquid

2 large jalapeños, diced

2 teaspoons minced garlic

2 teaspoons seasoning salt

2 pounds boneless, skinless chicken thighs

8 to 10 slices bacon

2 teaspoons paprika

2 teaspoons herbes de Provence

Orzo Rice Pilaf (page 178), for serving

+ Preheat the oven to 400 degrees F. Line a 9-by-13-inch baking dish with aluminum foil.

+ In a medium bowl, mash and stir the cream cheese and sour cream together until well combined. Add the pepper jack cheese, spinach, jalapeños, garlic, and seasoning salt. Mash and stir until well combined.

+ Scoop 2 to 3 tablespoons of the cream cheese mixture into the center of each chicken thigh, then roll it up and wrap with a bacon slice to hold it closed.

+ Place the rolled chicken thighs in the prepared baking dish with the loose bacon ends facing down. Sprinkle with the paprika and herbes de Provence. Bake for 45 to 55 minutes, or until the bacon is crisp and the chicken is cooked through. Serve with the rice pilaf.

Best Damn Chicken and Dumplings

I didn't actually like chicken and dumplings when I was growing up. I thought it was boring. I only really came to like it as an adult when my mom's husband started making it for us. Then I started experimenting with a recipe that put my own take on the dish. For my chicken and dumplings, I use a whole chicken because I like the mix of white and dark meat. Having both kinds adds to the texture and gives this dish great flavor. I also make sure the chicken and broth are well seasoned. My only rule is that it can't be bland!

MAKES 10 SERVINGS

1 (4- to 5-pound) whole chicken, cleaned (see Cleaning Poultry 101 on page 140)

2½ teaspoons seasoning salt

3 sprigs of fresh thyme, leaves stripped

1 teaspoon ground black pepper

1 medium onion, finely minced

4 to 5 garlic cloves, minced

8 cups chicken broth

1 cup all-purpose flour, plus more for dusting

1 large egg, lightly beaten

1 tablespoon water

1 tablespoon salted butter, softened

1½ teaspoons kosher salt

½ cup heavy cream

1 teaspoon dried parsley flakes

◆ Place the chicken in a large pot and sprinkle with the seasoning salt, thyme leaves, and black pepper. Add the onion and garlic, then pour in the chicken broth and bring to a boil over medium-high heat. Reduce the heat to medium-low and simmer until the chicken is cooked through, about 1 hour.

◆ Meanwhile, in a large mixing bowl, combine the flour, egg, water, butter, and salt. Mix with a large fork until a ball of dough forms. Cover the bowl and refrigerate the dough until nice and cold, about 45 minutes.

- Knead the dough on a lightly floured surface, then roll it out into a 10-by-12-inch rectangle and cut into dumpling strips.

- When the chicken is done cooking, pull it out of the broth and let cool slightly, but leave the broth on the heat. Remove the skin and shred the meat from the bones. Discard the skin and bones.

- Turn the heat to medium-high and bring the broth to a boil. Add the dumplings and cook for 30 minutes. Pour in the cream, add the chicken meat and parsley flakes, and stir. Cook for 10 minutes. Serve and enjoy!

Easy Smoked Whole Turkey

My husband likes turkey, but he doesn't care for plain turkey. He does however love this smoked version, which infuses the bird with amazing flavor. I bump it up even more by rubbing seasoned butter under the skin. The butter also keeps the turkey juicy and moist without any brining.

I smoke a lot of foods, so I have an electric pellet smoker that takes a lot of the guesswork out of the process. Instead of using wood chips, I use wooden pellets. I prefer hickory, but feel free to use pecan or applewood or whatever wood you like.

MAKES 10 TO 12 SERVINGS

For the seasoned butter:
½ cup (1 stick) unsalted
    butter, softened
3 tablespoons extra-virgin olive oil
½ medium yellow onion, finely diced
5 garlic cloves, minced
2 teaspoons kosher salt
2 teaspoons poultry seasoning
1 teaspoon coarse black pepper
1 teaspoon grated lemon zest
½ teaspoon red pepper flakes

For the turkey:
Wood chips for smoking, soaked in
    water for 4 to 24 hours
1 (13- to 15-pound) whole turkey,
    cleaned (see Cleaning Poultry 101
    on page 140) and cavity emptied
3 tablespoons peanut oil or
    vegetable oil
2 teaspoons paprika
1½ teaspoons kosher salt
1½ teaspoons dried parsley flakes
1 teaspoon coarse black pepper

◆ First, make the seasoned butter. In a medium mixing bowl, combine all the seasoned butter ingredients. Using a whisk or handheld mixer, mix everything until well combined. Set aside.

◆ Prepare a charcoal grill or smoker for indirect heat at 275 degrees F. Sprinkle in the soaked wood chips.

◆ I start by doing a "walk around" with the turkey, meaning I make sure there isn't anything on the turkey that I don't want (excess fat, feathers, and, of course, I remove everything from the cavity!).

CONTINUED

- Using your hands or a rubber spatula, loosen the skin on the turkey. Rub the seasoned butter under the skin as well as inside the cavity. Next, drizzle the oil all over the turkey, then sprinkle with the paprika, salt, parsley flakes, and black pepper. Rub the turkey down to ensure it's seasoned all over.

- Carefully place the turkey on the center of the grill or smoker and close the lid. Smoke the turkey for 6 to 7 hours, or until the internal temperature reaches at least 165 degrees F.

- Remove from the grill or smoker and let the turkey rest for 30 minutes before cutting into it. Serve and enjoy!

Cleaning Poultry 101

I like to clean most of my meats, especially poultry, with 2 cups water mixed with 2 teaspoons apple cider vinegar or lemon juice. If you see anything on the poultry that looks like it's not supposed to be there, pull it out or trim it. Gently rub and scrub the poultry with your fingers, rinse with the vinegar water, and repeat. Then pat dry with paper towels.

Slow Cooker Smothered Turkey Wings

FAN FAVE!

I love to smother things. I mean who wouldn't want their food just completely covered in a lip-smacking gravy? I also love all wings and do not sleep on turkey wings! They have so much flavor, and after a long simmer in the slow cooker, they become falling-off-the-bone tender.

This is a great foolproof recipe for Thanksgiving if you're feeding a smaller group and don't want to commit to a whole turkey. Making it in the slow cooker means you don't have to babysit the dish. It'll also free up the oven for your sides. So overall, this is a win-win (or wing-wing? LOL!).

MAKES 4 SERVINGS

½ cup all-purpose flour
1 tablespoon seasoning salt
1 tablespoon onion powder
1 tablespoon garlic powder
1½ teaspoons dried thyme
1½ teaspoons celery seed
2 large turkey wings, cleaned
   (see Cleaning Poultry 101 on page
   140) and separated into flats,
   drumettes, and tips

¾ cup vegetable oil, divided
1 large red onion, diced
1 large portobello mushroom, diced
6 cups regular or low-sodium chicken
   or turkey broth
4 to 5 fresh sage leaves, chopped
Cooked long-grain white rice or
   mashed potatoes and greens,
   for serving

◆ In a large mixing bowl, combine the flour with the seasoning salt, onion powder, garlic powder, thyme, and celery seed and whisk to combine.

◆ Coat the turkey wings with the seasoned flour, then let sit for 5 to 10 minutes. Do not toss out the flour!

◆ Pour ½ cup of the vegetable oil into a large pan over medium heat. Once the oil is nice and hot, add the turkey in batches to avoid overcrowding the pan. Cook, flipping the turkey, until brown, 5 to 7 minutes. Remove the turkey from the pan and place in a slow cooker.

CONTINUED

- Next, toss the onion and mushroom into the pan and cook, stirring occasionally, until the onions are translucent, 2 to 3 minutes. Transfer the ingredients to the slow cooker.

- Pour the remaining ¼ cup vegetable oil into the pan and heat until nice and hot. Sprinkle in the reserved seasoned flour and cook, stirring constantly, until it is nice and brown. Carefully pour in the broth and whisk until nice and smooth. Add the sage and stir.

- Pour the gravy over the turkey wings. Cover the slow cooker and cook on low for 6 hours. Serve the turkey with rice or mashed potatoes and greens.

Deep-Fried Cornish Game Hens

FAN FAVE!

Cornish hens are like cute little chickens. They're younger than most of the chicken you find at the market, so they'll be that much more tender. Because they're smaller, they cook that much faster when whole.

I like to fry up these elegant birds for smaller holiday gatherings. It's important that you brine them beforehand. The brine and garlic-herb rub add a ton of flavor. Everyone loves the fried coating, but you don't want to disappoint guests with bland meat underneath. Brining will never let you down!

MAKES 2 SERVINGS

For the brine:
4 cups cold water
2 tablespoons sugar
1 tablespoon kosher salt

For the hens:
2 Cornish game hens, cleaned (see Cleaning Poultry 101 on page 140)
5 garlic cloves
2 sprigs of fresh marjoram, leaves stripped

1 (0.5–ounce) package fresh poultry blend herbs (rosemary, thyme, and sage)
2 teaspoons kosher salt
1 teaspoon ground black pepper
1 teaspoon cayenne pepper
1 cup self-rising flour
5 cups peanut oil or vegetable oil, for deep-frying

- In a large mixing bowl, combine the brine ingredients. Stir until the sugar and salt dissolve. Place the hens in the brine, cover, and refrigerate for 4 hours, or up to overnight.

- Remove the hens from the brine and pat dry, then cut out the backbones. Set the hens to the side.

- Using a mortar and pestle or mini food processor, grind the garlic, marjoram, and poultry herbs into a paste. Rub the hens with the paste, then season with the salt, black pepper, and cayenne.

CONTINUED

- Place the flour in a large paper or plastic bag. Working with one at a time, add a hen to the flour and shake the bag until it is coated all over. Remove from the bag and let the hens sit for 10 minutes.

- Next, pour the oil into a deep fryer or large pot and heat it to 360 degrees F.

- Fry 1 hen at a time, flipping once, until the outside is golden brown and there is no blood when you pierce down to the bone, about 15 minutes. Carefully remove the hen from the oil and transfer it to a wire rack to drain and rest before slicing. Repeat with the second hen. Serve with your pick of sides, because these pair well with everything!

Philly Cheesesteak Lasagna

FAN FAVE!

When I asked readers of my blog if they had any requests, I got huge responses for Philly cheesesteak as well as lasagna, so I decided to combine the two in one big decadent dish. This is a white lasagna, so there are no tomatoes. Instead, you'll find thinly sliced steak, bell peppers, and onions along with the noodles. They're layered with blankets of creamy white sauce, ricotta, and six other cheeses. (Like I said, this dish is de-ca-dent!) I use beef chuck flat iron steak. Depending on where you get your meat, it may cost a tad bit more than other steak, but I assure you it is so worth it. This cut is super tender and juicy and will make the overall dish that much more luxe.

MAKES 10 TO 12 SERVINGS

2 tablespoons vegetable oil, plus more for greasing

Kosher salt and ground black pepper

16 ounces lasagna noodles

4 pounds beef chuck flat iron steak, thinly sliced

1 large red bell pepper, sliced

1 large green bell pepper, sliced

1 large yellow onion, sliced

2 teaspoons minced garlic

¼ cup (½ stick) salted butter

⅓ cup all-purpose flour

1½ cups whole milk

8 ounces mascarpone cheese

¼ pound creamy Havarti cheese, cubed

16 ounces ricotta cheese

3 medium eggs

2 teaspoons Italian seasoning

16 ounces mozzarella cheese, shredded, divided

8 ounces provolone cheese, shredded

8 ounces white cheddar cheese, shredded

8 ounces Muenster cheese, shredded

- ◆ Preheat the oven to 350 degrees F. Lightly grease a 9-by-13-inch baking dish with vegetable oil.

- ◆ Bring a large pot of salted water to a boil and cook the lasagna noodles according to the package directions, then drain.

CONTINUED

- Meanwhile, pour the vegetable oil into a large skillet over medium-high heat. Once the oil is hot, add the steak and season with salt and pepper. Cook, stirring occasionally, until the steak is no longer pink, about 5 minutes. Transfer the steak to a cutting board and, when cool enough to handle, chop it into bite-size pieces. Transfer the steak to a medium bowl.

- Add the bell peppers and onion to the skillet and season with salt and pepper. Cook over medium heat, stirring occasionally, until the onions are translucent, 3 to 5 minutes, then transfer the onions and peppers to the steak bowl.

- Toss the steak, onions, and peppers with the garlic, then set to the side.

- In a medium saucepan, melt the butter over medium heat. Sprinkle in the flour and cook, whisking continuously, for 2 minutes. Pour in the milk and whisk until there are no lumps. Next, whisk in the mascarpone, then the Havarti, until the cheeses are melted and the sauce is creamy. Reduce the heat to low.

- In another medium mixing bowl, combine the ricotta with the eggs, Italian seasoning, and half of the mozzarella. Stir with a rubber spatula until well combined. Set to the side.

- In a third medium bowl, toss together the remaining 8 ounces mozzarella with the provolone, cheddar, and Muenster.

- In the prepared baking dish, add a layer of lasagna noodles, then spread a layer of the ricotta mixture over the top. Add a layer of the shredded cheese mixture, then the steak mixture, then the cheese sauce. Repeat the layers again in the same order. Top the lasagna with a final layer of noodles, ricotta mixture, sauce, steak mixture, and shredded cheese.

- Bake the lasagna, uncovered, for 45 minutes. Let cool for about 10 minutes before digging in.

Easy Slow Cooker Short Ribs

FAN FAVE!

This recipe quickly became a popular fan fave after I showed clips on Instagram Stories. I was basically freestyling short ribs and people asked me to make a video. This took me by surprise. But Cousin Rosie is always down for her followers, so I decided to make this simple version for the slow cooker. Instead of making home-made gravy, I cheat with a packet of gravy. Throw everything in a slow cooker when you want something hearty but don't want to be in the kitchen forever and a day. The slow cooker is great for making tough cuts like short ribs tender. I happened to have ranch seasoning on hand for Mississippi pot roast, and I thought if it's good on pot roast, then it'd be good on short ribs—and it was!

MAKES 4 TO 6 SERVINGS

3 pounds bone-in beef short ribs

2 tablespoons extra-virgin olive oil

2 teaspoons seasoning salt or salt-free seasoning (I like salt-free Mrs. Dash)

2 or 3 large russet potatoes, peeled and chopped

1 pound carrots, peeled and chopped

2 large yellow onions, chopped

2 large red bell peppers, sliced

5 garlic cloves, chopped

1 (1-ounce) packet ranch seasoning

1 (0.87-ounce) packet brown gravy mix

3 bay leaves

1 sprig of fresh rosemary

1 sprig of fresh thyme

Chopped fresh parsley, for garnish

- Add the short ribs to a large bowl, then drizzle with the olive oil. Sprinkle the seasoning salt all over the ribs, then toss until well coated.

- In a large nonstick skillet over medium heat, cook the ribs, turning occasionally, until nice and browned, 2 to 3 minutes per side. Remove from the heat.

- Place the ribs, potatoes, carrots, onions, bell peppers, and garlic in a bowl or on a baking sheet. Sprinkle the ranch seasoning and gravy mix all over the ingredients.

- Toss everything except the potatoes into a 6-quart slow cooker. Add the potatoes, bay leaves, rosemary, and thyme on top of the other ingredients.

- Cover the slow cooker and cook on high for 6 hours. During the last hour of cooking, giving everything a nice stir. Once done, sprinkle the parsley on top and serve.

Jamaican Oxtails

One of my most popular videos on YouTube is for Jamaican oxtails, but since sharing that recipe, I've actually made a few changes—this is my new and improved version. I love Jamaican food, but we don't have many Caribbean restaurants in my area, so I had to learn how to make my favorite dishes at home. After traveling around and trying different variations, I came up with my own recipe.

The key to making these delicious Jamaican-style oxtails is using allspice, fresh thyme, and grated ginger. The traditional pepper to use is the scorching-hot Scotch bonnet, but I'm a punk when it comes to heat, so I swap it with a habanero. If you have a higher heat tolerance, go ahead and use the Scotch bonnet. Keep in mind, this recipe has long chilling and cooking times, so plan ahead!

MAKES 6 SERVINGS

2 pounds oxtails, fat trimmed

3 tablespoons store-bought browning sauce

2½ teaspoons seasoning salt

2 teaspoons ground allspice

1 teaspoon coarse black pepper

1 small yellow onion, diced

1 medium red bell pepper, diced

3 garlic cloves, minced

1 teaspoon grated fresh ginger

3 sprigs of fresh thyme

3 tablespoons vegetable oil

1 tablespoon all-purpose flour

4½ cups beef broth

1 large whole habanero pepper

1 (15-ounce) can lima beans, rinsed and drained

Pigeon Peas and Rice (page 177) or steamed rice, for serving

◆ Rinse the oxtails under cool water, then transfer them to a large bowl. Pour the browning sauce over the oxtails, then sprinkle with the seasoning salt, allspice, and black pepper. Add the onion, bell pepper, garlic, ginger, and thyme. Use your hands or tongs to toss everything together. Cover the bowl and refrigerate for 6 to 8 hours, or overnight.

◆ Pour the vegetable oil into a large pot over medium-high heat. Once the oil is hot, add the oxtails, onion, pepper, garlic, ginger, and thyme to the pot. Sprinkle in the flour and cook, stirring occasionally, until the oxtails are browned, 8 to 10 minutes.

◆ Next, pour in the beef broth and toss in the habanero. Cover and cook over medium heat until the oxtails are nice and tender, about 2½ hours. Add the lima beans to the pot, cover, and simmer for 30 more minutes.

◆ Serve with pigeon peas and rice.

Grilled Lamb Chops

These are not your ordinary lamb chops. The overnight marinade really amps up their flavor. The hot sauce, black pepper, and red pepper flakes contribute heat that's balanced by the honey. So they're not spicy but have just the right kick. The minced onion adds a great savoriness in the background. I make these on weekends when I want to fire up the grill. I like to cook my chops to medium-rare, but feel free to add a little more fire to yours.

MAKES 4 TO 6 SERVINGS

¼ cup extra-virgin olive oil

3 tablespoons mild hot sauce

3 tablespoons honey

1 small onion, minced

10 garlic cloves, minced

1 tablespoon seasoning salt

½ teaspoon coarse black pepper

½ teaspoon red pepper flakes (optional)

2 pounds thin lamb chops, patted dry

2 sprigs of fresh rosemary, leaves stripped and chopped

Nonstick cooking spray

◆ In a medium mixing bowl, whisk the olive oil, hot sauce, and honey until well combined. Stir in the onion, garlic, seasoning salt, black pepper, and red pepper flakes. Pour the marinade into a large freezer bag.

◆ Add the lamb and rosemary to the bag, and shake to distribute everything and coat the lamb. Refrigerate for a minimum of 4 hours, or overnight.

◆ Remove the bag from the refrigerator and let the lamb come to room temperature.

◆ Heat a large grill pan over medium-high heat until nice and hot. Spray with nonstick cooking spray. Grill a few lamb chops at a time until browned and grill marks appear, 8 to 9 minutes on each side. Transfer to a platter and serve with your favorite sides!

Cajun-Style Leg of Lamb

I love lamb, actually more than beef, and I like to spice it up. I can eat lamb the same way all the time—with Cajun seasoning. This makes my recipe different from other lamb dishes. Most of the flavor comes from the Cajun seasoning and garlic, and the fresh or dried thyme adds more depth to the dish, particularly because the flavors marry when the lamb marinates overnight.

This is a great dish for Easter or Christmas, as it offers a nice way to spice up the usual main dishes. It can make an impressive presentation, depending on how you dress it up on the platter.

MAKES 8 SERVINGS

1 (3–pound) bone-in leg of lamb

¼ cup extra-virgin olive oil, plus more for greasing

1 small red onion, minced

6 garlic cloves, minced

2 tablespoons Cajun seasoning

2 teaspoons minced fresh thyme leaves

2 teaspoons paprika

1½ teaspoons kosher salt

◆ Place the leg of lamb in a large freezer bag and set to the side.

◆ Place all the remaining ingredients in a food processor and pulse until well combined. Pour the oil mixture over the lamb. Seal the bag and refrigerate for at least 6 hours and up to 12 hours.

◆ Preheat the oven to 375 degrees F.

◆ Lightly grease a large roasting pan or rimmed baking sheet with olive oil, then add the lamb and the oil mixture to the pan. Cover with foil and bake for 1 hour.

◆ Remove from the oven and baste the lamb with the liquid from the pan, then return to the oven without the foil. Bake, uncovered, for 30 minutes more, or until the lamb has a golden-brown crust and is cooked medium-rare to medium, depending on your preference. Serve with your side of choice.

Stuffed Pork Chops

If I ever have leftover rice or dressing, I use it up by stuffing pork chops or Cornish hens or chicken breasts. When I was dreaming up this recipe, I happened to have cornbread dressing with collards and smoked turkey, and I thought to myself it might be so good stuffed into pork chops. Happy to report, it turned out soooo good! The smokiness from the turkey seasons the pork from the inside out. All you need on the outside is onion powder, salt, and pepper.

I prefer bone-in chops because the bone adds flavor to the meat, but you could use boneless. Make sure you use a thick cut to hold the filling; plus, it won't dry out during cooking. I spread the dressing on the bottom of the baking dish and then set the chops on top because the drippings flavor the dressing even more. Make a full batch of dressing if you want to have extra!

MAKES 8 SERVINGS

3 tablespoons extra-virgin olive oil, plus more for greasing	1 teaspoon ground black pepper
2 teaspoons garlic salt	½ teaspoon red pepper flakes
2 teaspoons onion powder	8 large thick-cut bone-in pork chops (about 4 pounds)
2 teaspoons dried parsley flakes	½ batch unbaked Collard Green and Smoked Turkey Dressing (page 168)
2 teaspoons Creole seasoning	

◆ Preheat the oven to 375 degrees F. Lightly grease a large baking dish with olive oil.

◆ In a small bowl, combine the garlic salt, onion powder, parsley flakes, Creole seasoning, black pepper, and red pepper flakes. Stir and set to the side.

◆ Place the pork chops on a flat surface, then cut a horizontal pocket in the side of each chop about 2 inches deep. Drizzle the oil all over the chops, then sprinkle the seasoning all over the chops.

◆ Stuff the pork chops with some of the dressing. Add the remaining dressing to the prepared baking dish. Place the chops on top of the dressing, then cover the baking dish with foil.

◆ Bake for 45 minutes, then remove the foil and bake for another 20 minutes, or until the chops are fully cooked throughout. Serve and enjoy!

Blackberry-Glazed Ribs

I love ribs! I like them grilled, baked, smothered, and glazed. I love sweet and sticky glaze on my pork ribs, so it's no wonder why these blackberry-glazed ribs are one of my favorites. The glaze is a combination of blackberries, brown sugar, and a few pantry staples. The sweet fruity glaze is simply amazing on ribs—and also tastes great on chicken!

I always have blackberries on hand and in my freezer. It feels like we have blackberry bushes on every block. There are so many in the Pacific Northwest. They freeze well, and when you miss summertime, it's easy to thaw some out for these ribs! If you don't live in the Northwest and they are harder to come by, check out the freezer section at your local grocery store.

MAKES 8 SERVINGS

For the ribs:
1 tablespoon seasoning salt
2½ teaspoons onion powder
2 teaspoons garlic salt
2 teaspoons paprika
1 teaspoon red pepper flakes
1 teaspoon ground black pepper
5 pounds pork ribs,
   membranes removed
3 tablespoons extra-virgin olive oil

For the blackberry glaze:
6 ounces fresh blackberries
½ cup barbecue sauce of your choice
½ cup blackberry jam
¼ cup water
2 tablespoons light brown sugar
1 tablespoon red wine vinegar
2 teaspoons extra-virgin olive oil

◆ Preheat the oven to 375 degrees F.

◆ In a small bowl, combine the seasoning salt, onion powder, garlic salt, paprika, red pepper flakes, and black pepper. Stir well, then set to the side.

◆ Place the ribs on a flat surface and drizzle with the olive oil. Rub the oil all over the ribs. Next, generously season the ribs with the seasoning mixture, making sure to get both sides.

◆ Place the ribs in a baking dish or rimmed baking sheet, cover with foil, and bake for 1 hour.

- Meanwhile, make the blackberry glaze. Combine all the glaze ingredients in a medium saucepan over medium heat. Mash the blackberries and cook until thickened, about 15 minutes. Remove the saucepan from the heat and set to the side.

- Remove the baking dish from the oven and pull off the foil. Heavily brush the blackberry glaze on both sides of the ribs.

- Bake the ribs, uncovered, for 30 more minutes. Remove the ribs from the oven and let cool. Serve with cornbread and greens, or any of your favorite sides.

Slow Cooker Neck Bones and Potatoes

FAN FAVE!

I know a lot of cousins love smothered oxtails but not the oxtail price; this recipe is a way to mimic that dish without spending a lot of money. I am so grateful my mama taught me how to swap out more expensive cuts for more affordable cuts of meat. I grew up eating neck bones because when my single mom was in college, she had to pinch pennies. Neck bones have great flavor, and the meat gets super tender in the slow cooker. The gravy is wonderful with the potatoes.

While I like pork neck bones, you can use beef neck bones instead. For the cousins out there who are intimidated by making gravy, I got you! This recipe uses packaged gravy mix as a shortcut for instant flavor.

MAKES 6 SERVINGS

3 pounds fresh pork neck bones (not smoked)
1 tablespoon seasoning salt
2 teaspoons garlic powder
2 teaspoons onion powder
1½ teaspoons coarse black pepper
2 (0.87–ounce) packets brown gravy mix

1½ large yellow onions, sliced
3 cups regular or low-sodium vegetable broth
5 medium russet potatoes, peeled and cut into large pieces
Soulful Cabbage and Collard Greens (page 164), for serving

◆ Make sure that you clean the neck bones before anything else (don't skip this step!). Once cleaned, toss them into a 6–quart slow cooker.

◆ Sprinkle the neck bones with the seasoning salt, garlic powder, onion powder, and black pepper, followed by the gravy mix. Add the onions and stir everything together. Pour in the vegetable broth and toss in the potatoes.

◆ Cover the slow cooker and cook on high for 6 hours. Serve with the cabbage and collards or your vegetable side of choice.

Side Pieces

Soulful Cabbage and Collard Greens 164

Creamed Spinach with Bacon 166

Southern Broccoli Casserole 167

Collard Green and Smoked Turkey Dressing 168

Creamy Mashed Baby Reds 170

Roasted Parsnips with Bacon 172

Creole Street Corn 173

Fresh Creamed Corn 175

Corn Pudding Casserole 176

Pigeon Peas and Rice 177

White Beans and Sausage 179

Orzo Rice Pilaf 180

Southern Baked Macaroni and Cheese
   Casserole 182

Soulful Cabbage and Collard Greens

People get bored by the same ol' cabbage or the same ol' collards, so I thought, "Why not mix the two together?" The combo works beautifully because on their own, collards can be bitter, so the cabbage balances them out with some mild sweetness. My husband loves his collards, and my son absolutely loves his cabbage. When I mix the two, both men in my life get the taste they love and I'm happy they are eating their greens!

Make sure that you wash the cabbage and collard greens before anything else (see Prepping Greens 101 on page 21). I cook the vegetables with regular bacon. When I make greens or cabbage, I usually use ham hocks, smoked turkey, or even neck bone, but bacon works great here and cooks a lot faster than the other meats! Serve alongside fried chicken or catfish, potato salad, and especially cornbread.

MAKES 6 SERVINGS

1 pound bacon, chopped

1 large yellow, white, or red onion, diced

1 large red bell pepper, diced

1 large head of green cabbage, cored and sliced

2 pounds collard greens, ribs removed, leaves chopped

1½ cups water

1 tablespoon minced garlic

2 teaspoons seasoning salt

1½ teaspoons coarse black pepper

Pinch of red pepper flakes (optional)

◆ Place a large pot over medium-high heat, then toss in the bacon. Cook, stirring occasionally, until the bacon browns a bit, 4 to 5 minutes. Then toss in the onion and bell pepper, and continue to cook, stirring occasionally, until they start to soften, about 2 minutes.

◆ Fold in the cabbage and collards. Add the water and garlic, then sprinkle in the seasoning salt, black pepper, and red pepper flakes. Give everything a nice stir.

◆ Reduce the heat to medium, cover, and cook, stirring occasionally, until the cabbage and collards are nice and tender, about 45 minutes.

Creamed Spinach with Bacon

This is the most delicious, rich dish you could ever make with frozen spinach. I grew up eating a lot of spinach because I was one of those rare kids who liked it. And because I'm anemic, spinach, along with beets, are good for me. They're still my favorite. But even if you're not a spinach fan, the bacon jazzes up the recipe to make it absolutely irresistible. The cream cheese makes it thick and creamy.

I love this as a side for steak with Creamy Mashed Baby Reds (page 170). For an extra-special treat, use it as a topping for the Loaded Baked Oysters (page 66).

MAKES 6 SERVINGS

1 pound frozen chopped spinach, thawed	1 tablespoon cream cheese, softened
4 slices thick-cut bacon	2 teaspoons seasoning salt
2 tablespoons salted butter	2 teaspoons onion powder
3 tablespoons all-purpose flour	½ teaspoon ground black pepper
2 cups half-and-half	¼ teaspoon red pepper flakes
4 garlic cloves, minced	¼ teaspoon ground nutmeg
	½ cup grated Parmesan cheese

◆ Wrap the spinach in a cheesecloth and squeeze out all the excess liquid. Set it to the side.

◆ Place a large skillet over medium heat, then add the bacon and cook, flipping once, until it's nice and crisp, 7 to 8 minutes. Transfer the bacon to a paper-towel-lined plate and let cool.

◆ Leave the rendered fat in the skillet over medium heat, then add the butter and let it melt. Sprinkle in the flour and cook, stirring, until the raw flour smell is gone, about 2 minutes. Pour in the half-and-half and stir until well combined.

◆ Crumble in the bacon, add the garlic and cream cheese, and stir. Sprinkle in the seasoning salt, onion powder, black pepper, red pepper flakes, and nutmeg. Stir and then bring to a boil. Turn the heat down to medium again and cook until the sauce thickens, 4 to 5 minutes.

◆ Stir in the spinach. Add the Parmesan and stir everything until well combined. Cook until thickened to your liking, 5 to 7 minutes, then serve.

Southern Broccoli Casserole

There are a lot of broccoli casseroles out there. I make mine with a homemade cream sauce and lots of cheese, specifically sharp cheddar. Not only is it my favorite, but it pairs well with broccoli. I like to use frozen broccoli that's already chopped, because it's less expensive than fresh and you won't get broccoli fluff all over your counter. I top my casserole with crushed Ritz crackers, but you can leave them out if you don't want that crunch. I personally can't skip it; it really is the best topping.

Broccoli casserole is a great dish to get veggies into your kids—it's creamy, the broccoli is mild, and the sharp cheddar really shines through. And it's a perfect crowd-pleaser for serving up when you haven't hit the grocery store since everything the recipe calls for is a pantry staple.

MAKES 6 TO 8 SERVINGS

3½ tablespoons salted butter, divided, plus more for greasing
2 large eggs, beaten
1 cup mayonnaise
1½ cups shredded sharp cheddar cheese
2½ teaspoons seasoning salt
1 teaspoon ground black pepper

1 (20-ounce) bag frozen chopped broccoli
3 garlic cloves, minced
1 small onion, diced
1½ tablespoons all-purpose flour
2½ cups half-and-half
1 sleeve of Ritz crackers, crushed

- Preheat the oven to 350 degrees F. Lightly butter a 4-quart casserole dish.

- In a large mixing bowl, combine the eggs, mayonnaise, cheddar cheese, seasoning salt, and pepper and mix well. Stir in the broccoli and garlic, then set aside.

- In a medium saucepan, melt 1½ tablespoons of the butter over medium heat. Add the onion and cook, stirring, until the onions are translucent, 3 to 4 minutes. Add the flour and cook, stirring, until the raw flour smell is gone, about 3 minutes.

- Pour in the half-and-half and cook, whisking occasionally to prevent lumps, until the sauce thickens, about 5 minutes. Fold the sauce into the broccoli mixture, then pour everything into the prepared casserole dish.

- Top the casserole with the crackers. Dice the remaining 2 tablespoons butter into small pieces and scatter over the top. Bake, uncovered, for 30 minutes, or until golden brown. Let cool slightly before serving.

Collard Green and Smoked Turkey Dressing

Every Thanksgiving it seems like the same ol' side dishes are served. You know: stuffing, mashed potatoes, and green bean casserole. Don't get me wrong, I love them all, but I like to spice up my menu. This recipe is a twist on the traditional cornbread stuffing—or what we call "dressing" in my family because we never stuffed it into the bird.

The idea came about because I would mix all my favorite Thanksgiving dishes on my plate. So I decided to make a dressing that combines collards and smoked turkey with the cornbread. For Thanksgiving, I make two dressings: my regular Southern-style dressing for those who want something traditional, and this one for the more adventurous spirits.

MAKES 12 SERVINGS

1½ pounds smoked turkey leg or wing

6 cups regular or low-sodium turkey broth

½ cup (1 stick) unsalted butter, divided, plus more for greasing

2 stalks celery, diced

1 medium red bell pepper, diced

1 medium yellow onion, diced

1 tablespoon minced garlic

1 teaspoon kosher salt

1 teaspoon ground black pepper

1 (10-ounce) bag collard greens, stems removed, leaves chopped (And thoroughly cleaned! See Prepping Greens 101 on page 21.)

2 (24-ounce) bags herb cornbread dressing

1 teaspoon ground sage

1 teaspoon dried thyme

¼ teaspoon red pepper flakes

- In a 6-quart slow cooker, combine the smoked turkey with the turkey broth. Cover the slow cooker and cook on high for 3 hours.

- Remove the turkey from the slow cooker, reserving 6 cups of the broth, then shred the meat and set both aside.

- Preheat the oven to 350 degrees F. Butter a 9-by-13-inch baking dish.

- In a large skillet, melt 4 tablespoons of the butter over medium heat, then toss in the celery, bell pepper, onion, and garlic. Add the salt and black pepper, and cook, stirring occasionally, until the onions are translucent, 2 to 3 minutes. Transfer the veggies to a large bowl and set aside.

- In the same skillet, toss in the collards and cook, stirring occasionally, until tender, about 5 minutes. Transfer the greens to the large bowl.

- In the same skillet, melt the remaining 4 tablespoons butter. In a large mixing bowl, combine the cornbread dressing with the reserved broth and the melted butter. Let sit for 15 minutes to soak up all the flavor.

- Next, fold the cooked veggie mixture and shredded turkey into the cornbread dressing. Sprinkle in the sage, thyme, and red pepper flakes, and fold once more. Transfer the dressing to the prepared baking dish.

- Cover the dish with aluminum foil and bake for 50 minutes. Once done, remove from the oven, and let sit for 10 minutes before serving.

Creamy Mashed Baby Reds

Why do I use baby red potatoes for this mash? Because they're creamier, easier to mash, and as an added bonus, they have a thin skin that you don't have to peel! Anytime I can save time and boost flavor, I'm signing up. Stay away from russet potatoes here—they don't have the same texture. My secret to making these mashed potatoes even richer is cream cheese—it adds to the flavor without watering down the dish like milk would.

This is a great side for a lot of mains, but I particularly like it with the Blackened Salmon (page 127). You may never peel a potato again if you stick to these creamy mashed baby reds!

MAKES 8 SERVINGS

2 pounds baby red potatoes, scrubbed	½ cup (1 stick) salted butter, at room temperature, plus more for serving
6 cups vegetable broth	2 ounces cream cheese, at room temperature
2 cups water	2 teaspoons kosher salt
½ cup half-and-half	Chopped fresh parsley, for garnish

◆ In a large pot, combine the potatoes with the vegetable broth and water. Bring to a boil and cook over high heat until the potatoes are fork-tender, about 25 minutes.

◆ Drain all the liquid from the pot, then place the pot over medium-low heat. Mash the potatoes with a potato masher, then add the half-and-half, butter, cream cheese, and salt. Fold until everything is well combined, then remove from the heat.

◆ Plate the mashed potatoes, top with more butter, if desired, and sprinkle parsley on top.

Roasted Parsnips with Bacon

Before I really knew what a parsnip was, I called it a big white carrot. Then a sponsor of my blog introduced me to a farm, where Farmer Ray showed me around. He presented me with parsnips pulled right out of the dirt. I had no idea how to cook them, so Farmer Ray suggested I roast them. I added my own spin with my favorite seasonings and really loved the flavor. Parsnips kind of taste like a combo of potato and carrot with a little bit of turnip. You can cook them in different ways, but roasting gives them a great texture.

MAKES 8 SERVINGS

Vegetable oil, for greasing
¼ pound bacon
2 pounds parsnips, peeled
   and chopped
2½ teaspoons seasoning salt
2 teaspoons herbes de Provence

2 teaspoons garlic powder
2 teaspoons onion powder
½ teaspoon coarse black pepper
½ teaspoon cayenne pepper
Chopped fresh parsley, for garnish

- Preheat the oven to 400 degrees F. Lightly grease a 9-by-13-inch baking sheet.

- Place a large skillet over medium heat, then add the bacon and cook, flipping once, until it's nice and crisp, about 5 minutes. Transfer the bacon to a paper-towel-lined plate and set aside to cool, but reserve the rendered fat.

- Toss the parsnips into a large plastic freezer bag. Drizzle in the bacon fat and sprinkle in the seasoning salt, herbes de Provence, garlic powder, onion powder, black pepper, and cayenne. Shake the bag, then transfer the parsnips to the prepared baking sheet, spacing them apart.

- Bake for 25 minutes, or until the parsnips are tender. Remove from the oven, crumble the bacon all over, and garnish with parsley. Serve and enjoy!

Creole Street Corn

I didn't think it was possible for anyone to love corn more than I do, but my neighbor is that person. Every summer, especially around the Fourth of July, he makes Mexican street corn, and I am into it. One time, when I tried to make Mexican street corn myself, I didn't have the right chili powder, so I used Creole seasoning instead. It added the spiciness but also gave the corn a hit of black pepper, dried herbs, and lingering smokiness. Definitely give it a try if you like Mexican street corn. This may become your new favorite.

MAKES 6 SERVINGS

3 tablespoons salted butter, melted

6 ears of corn, husks and silk removed

2 teaspoons Creole seasoning, divided

1 teaspoon coarse black pepper

1 cup Mexican crema

½ cup mayonnaise

3 tablespoons freshly squeezed lime juice

⅓ cup grated Parmesan cheese

¼ cup finely chopped fresh parsley

2 tablespoons chopped fresh cilantro

½ teaspoon red pepper flakes

- Preheat a grill to 350 degrees F.

- Brush the butter all over the corn, then sprinkle with 1 teaspoon of the Creole seasoning and the black pepper.

- Wrap each ear of corn in aluminum foil, place on the grill, and close the lid. Grill until the corn is tender, about 25 minutes. Unwrap the corn.

- In a small bowl, stir the crema, mayonnaise, and lime juice until well combined. Brush the mixture onto the ears of corn, then sprinkle with the remaining 1 teaspoon Creole seasoning, Parmesan, parsley, cilantro, and red pepper flakes. Serve and enjoy!

Fresh Creamed Corn

Creamed corn was my favorite as a kid. When I was younger, my mom used canned creamed corn, but when I got older, I started making it myself. For this recipe you'll need fresh corn, so don't try to cheat with the canned or frozen stuff. I also use half-and-half instead of milk to make the dish richer. If your corn isn't sweet enough, you can compensate with a little more sugar.

MAKES 4 SERVINGS

4 ears of corn, husks and silk removed, cobs rinsed with cool water

2 tablespoons bacon fat

1 tablespoon all-purpose flour

½ cup half-and-half, or ¼ cup milk plus ¼ cup heavy cream

1½ tablespoons sugar

½ teaspoon kosher salt

¼ teaspoon ground black pepper

◆ Using a sharp knife, cut the corn kernels from the cobs and set aside.

◆ In a large pan over medium heat, add the bacon fat. Once the grease is nice and hot, toss in the corn, and cook, stirring occasionally, until tender, about 5 minutes.

◆ Sprinkle in the flour and cook, stirring, until the raw flour smell is gone, 2 to 3 minutes. Pour in the half-and-half and stir until well incorporated.

◆ Sprinkle in the sugar, salt, and pepper. Stir and cook until the creamed corn thickens to your preference, 10 to 15 minutes. Serve and enjoy!

Corn Pudding Casserole

People make corn pudding many different ways, and here's mine: it's like buttery creamed corn crossed with cornbread batter and baked until golden brown. Serve the dish warm while it still has a soft pudding-like texture. To make it even easier, I use store-bought cornbread mix and canned corn as shortcuts.

The result is a sweet, rich side dish that pairs amazingly well with savory mains, the way candied yams do. My favorite way is to serve it with ham, which has the saltiness to counter the pudding's sweetness. I make this casserole for holiday gatherings because it wows everyone at the table (and otherwise, I might eat the whole thing myself!).

MAKES 12 SERVINGS

1 cup (2 sticks) unsalted butter, melted, plus more for greasing

4 large eggs

2 (15-ounce) cans creamed corn

1 (15-ounce) can whole kernel corn, drained

½ cup sugar

1 teaspoon vanilla extract

⅛ teaspoon ground nutmeg

1 cup sour cream

1 (8.5-ounce) package sweet cornbread mix

◆ Preheat the oven to 350 degrees F. Butter a 9-by-13-inch baking dish.

◆ In a large mixing bowl, beat the eggs until they're one color. Add the creamed corn and whole kernel corn. Stir until well combined, then add the sugar, vanilla, and nutmeg. Stir again until well combined.

◆ Mix or fold in the sour cream. Pour in the melted butter, then sprinkle in the cornbread mix. Stir everything until well incorporated, then scrape the batter into the prepared baking dish.

◆ Bake for 35 to 40 minutes, or until golden brown on top and just jiggly. Remove from the oven and let sit for 5 to 7 minutes before serving.

Pigeon Peas and Rice

Pigeon peas and rice is a classic Jamaican side dish that's fragrant with coconut milk, allspice, and thyme, with a kick of chili heat. I got the recipe many years ago (from a former coworker, I think?), but I've since tweaked a lot of the ingredients. I use canned pigeon peas instead of dried to speed up the process, vegetable broth instead of water to amp up the flavor, and jalapeño instead of a Scotch bonnet because I can't handle all that heat.

This is the traditional side to Jamaican Oxtails (page 152), but you can also pair it with other dishes, like fried plantains, cornbread (pages 86 and 88), or Soulful Cabbage and Collard Greens (page 164).

MAKES 8 SERVINGS

1 (13.5-ounce) can coconut milk

2½ cups low-sodium vegetable broth

1 (15-ounce) can pigeon peas, rinsed and drained

1 small onion, diced

1 large jalapeño (seeded, if you prefer less heat), diced

2 teaspoons minced garlic

2 sprigs of fresh thyme

1 teaspoon seasoning salt

¼ teaspoon ground allspice

3 cups long-grain white rice, rinsed and drained

◆ Pour the coconut milk and vegetable broth into a large pot. Add the pigeon peas, onion, jalapeño, garlic, thyme, seasoning salt, and allspice. Bring to a boil over medium-high heat and cook, stirring occasionally, for 5 minutes.

◆ Add the rice and cover the pot. Reduce the heat to low and cook for 40 to 45 minutes, or until the rice is tender. Fluff the peas and rice with a fork. Serve and enjoy!

White Beans and Sausage

When I was growing up, we did not have a lot of money, so we always had dried beans (white, red, pinto). Dried beans are affordable and packed with flavor and protein. Making beans was something I had to know how to do growing up. When my mom worked, I was in charge of dinner.

With white beans, I prefer to make them with andouille sausage, but other smoked sausage, such as beef, works. This is an any-weather dish. No matter what time of year, you can enjoy beans and sausage. Pair it with Deep-Fried Cornish Game Hens (page 145), hot sauce, and greens for a complete meal. You could eat it on its own, but in most soul food households you're not going to. You're going to soak up that creamy goodness with greens and cornbread.

MAKES 8 SERVINGS

16 ounces dried white beans

2 teaspoons vegetable oil

1 pound andouille sausage, sliced into
   ¼-inch pieces

1 medium red onion, diced

8 cups chicken broth, divided

2 teaspoons Creole seasoning

1½ teaspoons dried thyme

1 teaspoon cayenne pepper

½ teaspoon red pepper flakes

½ teaspoon ground black pepper

4 cups cooked long-grain white rice

Chopped green onions and paprika,
   for garnish

- Start by sorting and rinsing the beans (see Sorting Beans 101 on page 19). Then put the beans into a medium pot and pour enough water in to cover them. Place the pot over high heat and boil for 2 minutes. Turn off the heat and let sit for 10 minutes.

- In a large pot over medium heat, add the vegetable oil and andouille sausage. Cook for 5 minutes to brown. Add the red onion and cook until it starts to sweat. Pour in 6 cups of the chicken broth and increase the heat to medium-high.

- Drain the water from the beans, then add them to the large pot, stirring to incorporate. Cook for 30 minutes, then add the remaining 2 cups of broth.

- Sprinkle in the Creole seasoning, thyme, cayenne, red pepper flakes, and black pepper. Reduce the heat to medium, stir the beans, and cover the pot. Cook for another 45 minutes.

- Stir the beans, taste for doneness, then spoon into bowls. Add some rice on top of the beans in the center of the bowl, then add more beans. Garnish with green onions and paprika before serving with cornbread.

Orzo Rice Pilaf

If you're looking for an ideal side dish that's a blank canvas for mains, this is it. My mom always made her rice pilaf with orzo, and I see a similar version on the menus at the soul food restaurants in my area. While this recipe works as a blank canvas, it's by no means bland!

I like to serve this pilaf with meatloaf, Grilled Lamb Chops (page 155), Bacon-Wrapped Stuffed Chicken Thighs (page 134), or Jamaican Jerk Shrimp and Peppers (page 124).

MAKES 6 SERVINGS

2 tablespoons extra-virgin olive oil
1 tablespoon salted butter
¼ cup minced yellow onion
¾ cup orzo
¾ cup long-grain white rice, rinsed
   until the water runs clear

3 cups chicken broth
1 tablespoon minced garlic
2 teaspoons seasoning salt
½ teaspoon ground thyme
2 teaspoons chopped fresh parsley,
   for garnish (optional)

◆ In a large saucepan over medium-high heat, combine the oil and butter. Once the butter is melted, add the onion and cook for 1 minute, stirring occasionally. Stir in the orzo, and cook, stirring occasionally, until it is golden brown, about 2 minutes. Add the rice and cook, stirring occasionally, for 2 minutes.

◆ Next, add the chicken broth, garlic, seasoning salt, and thyme and stir. Bring to a simmer, then turn the heat to low, cover, and cook for 15 to 20 minutes, or until the rice is tender and the broth is absorbed.

◆ Fluff the rice with a fork and garnish with the parsley.

Southern Baked Macaroni and Cheese Casserole

This mac and cheese casserole is the creamiest, cheesiest, best-ever recipe (drops the mic and walks away). I'm not playing y'all! And guess what? It calls for only two different cheeses that are easy to find: sharp cheddar for the flavor and mozzarella for the gooeyness. No more searching for obscure cheeses. I got you covered with this one.

What makes this version different from my other mac and cheese recipes is the crispy crust. I also layer the casserole with cheese on the bottom and top (and plenty of cheese in between!) so it's like a cheese-crusted sandwich when you slice into it.

MAKES 12 SERVINGS

6 tablespoons salted butter, divided, plus more for greasing

1 teaspoon kosher salt, for boiling the pasta

3 cups uncooked elbow macaroni

3 tablespoons all-purpose flour

3½ cups half-and-half

16 ounces sharp cheddar cheese shredded, divided

2 teaspoons seasoning salt

1 teaspoon ground black pepper

8 ounces mozzarella cheese, shredded

½ cup Italian-style panko bread crumbs

◆ Preheat the oven to 350 degrees F. Butter a 9-by-13-inch baking dish.

◆ In a large pot over high heat, bring about 2 quarts of water to a boil and sprinkle in the kosher salt. Add the macaroni and cook until it is al dente (cooked but still firm). Drain the pasta and transfer it to a large mixing bowl.

◆ While the pasta is cooking, melt 4 tablespoons of the butter in a large saucepan over medium heat. Sprinkle in the flour and whisk until there are no lumps. Pour in the half-and-half and whisk until smooth. Cook until the mixture starts to thicken, then reduce the heat to medium-low.

◆ Add 8 ounces of the cheddar cheese and whisk until well incorporated. Sprinkle in the seasoning salt and black pepper and stir. Pour the cheese sauce over the cooked macaroni and fold it in until well incorporated.

- In a small bowl, toss the remaining 8 ounces cheddar with the mozzarella. Sprinkle a layer of this mozzarella mixture on the bottom of the prepared baking dish, then top with a heavy layer of macaroni and cheese. Repeat, finishing with a final layer of the mozzarella mixture.

- In a small saucepan or microwaveable bowl, melt the remaining 2 tablespoons butter. Add the bread crumbs and stir. Sprinkle the mixture over the casserole.

- Bake, uncovered, for 25 to 30 minutes, or until the bread crumbs are golden brown and crisp. Serve and enjoy the best-ever Southern baked macaroni and cheese casserole!!

Somethin' Sweet

Southern Tea Cakes   186

Better-Than-Sex Cookies   188

Rolo Brownies   191

Salted Caramel and Chocolate Chip Cookies   192

King Cake   193

Peach Cobbler Bread Pudding   197

Cherries and Cream Funnel Cakes   198

Blackberry Pie   199

Chocolate Chess Pie   203

Chocolate Cornbread Cheesecake   204

Strawberry Shortcake Cheesecake   207

Caramel Cake   210

Coconut Cake   213

Moist 7UP Cake   215

The Ultimate Carrot Cake   218

Three-Layer Key Lime Cake with
   Key Lime Buttercream Frosting   220

Southern Tea Cakes

Tea cakes are like sugar cookies but with a hint of nutmeg. They have a mild flavor that goes great with tea, hence the name. Rumor has it that my great-grandmother Bee (not to be confused with her daughter Rosa Mae!) was not much of a cook but she made the best tea cakes. Unfortunately, she passed before I could learn her recipe. It took me about ten years to approach something close to her version and get the stamp of approval from family members, but I finally nailed it.

MAKES ABOUT 24 TEA CAKES

Nonstick baking spray

4 cups all-purpose flour, plus more for dusting

2 teaspoons baking powder

1 teaspoon baking soda

½ teaspoon ground nutmeg

½ teaspoon kosher salt

½ cup (1 stick) unsalted butter, softened

½ cup butter-flavored shortening

1 cup granulated sugar

1 cup light brown sugar

2 large eggs

½ cup buttermilk

1 tablespoon freshly squeezed lemon juice

2½ teaspoons vanilla extract

* Preheat the oven to 350 degrees F. Place a baking mat on a baking sheet (or skip the mat, it's up to you) and spray it with baking spray.

* In a large mixing bowl, sift or whisk together the flour, baking powder, baking soda, nutmeg, and salt until well combined, then set to the side.

* In a separate large mixing bowl, using a handheld mixer with the dough hook attachment, combine the butter and shortening and mix well. Add both sugars and mix well on medium speed, then add the eggs and mix on medium speed until well combined. Next, add the buttermilk, lemon juice, and vanilla, and mix on medium speed until fully incorporated.

* Gradually add the dry ingredients to the wet ingredients, mixing on medium speed until everything is well combined and a dough has formed.

- Transfer the dough to a lightly floured surface and roll out with a rolling pin to about ½ inch thick. Using 3½- to 4-inch cookie cutters, cut out your desired shapes, then transfer them to a baking sheet lined with wax paper. Chill the dough in the refrigerator for 10 minutes.

- Transfer as many of the tea cakes as will fit to the prepared sprayed baking sheet, leaving at least 1 inch between them. Bake the tea cakes for 7 to 8 minutes, or until golden on the edges.

- Remove the pan from the oven and transfer the tea cakes to a wire rack until they are cool to the touch. Bake the remaining tea cakes. Serve with tea or coffee.

Better-Than-Sex Cookies

Admit it, the title brought you here, and I'm not mad atcha! These cookies are definitely better than sex—and extremely addictive. I took some of my favorite sweets and turned them into amazing cookies. First we have the Oreos, which I can never resist. Then we have the Symphony bars that includes all of my favorites: the chocolate that reminds me of Kofi Siriboe, the toffee that reminds me of Method Man, and the almonds that . . . Well, you get the picture! Try these cookies, and serve them with some cold milk if you're really feeling kinky!

MAKES 2 DOZEN COOKIES

¾ cup (1½ sticks) unsalted
   butter, softened
¼ cup butter-flavored shortening
2 large eggs, at room temperature
1 cup packed light brown sugar
½ cup granulated sugar
2 teaspoons vanilla extract

½ teaspoon kosher salt
2½ cups all-purpose flour
¾ teaspoon baking soda
10 original Oreos, crumbled
2 extra-large Symphony bars with
   almonds and toffee chips, chopped
Vegetable oil, for greasing

◆ In a large mixing bowl, using a handheld mixer, mix the butter, shortening, and eggs on medium speed. Add the brown sugar, granulated sugar, vanilla, and salt. Mix until well combined. Change the attachment to the dough hook.

◆ In a medium bowl, whisk together the flour and baking soda. Gradually add the dry ingredients to the wet ingredients, and mix on low speed until well combined. Add the Oreos and Symphony pieces and mix or fold in. Wrap the bowl with plastic wrap and refrigerate for 2 hours.

◆ Preheat the oven to 350 degrees F. Lightly grease a baking sheet.

◆ Scoop out the dough in 2-tablespoon mounds and place on the prepared baking sheet, leaving 2 inches of space between the cookies. Bake for 7 to 10 minutes, until the cookies are done.

◆ Transfer the cookies to a wire rack to cool. Repeat with the remaining cookie dough. Serve and enjoy! Like, *really* enjoy.

Rolo Brownies

Are you a chocoholic? Do you like caramel? Then you absolutely have to try these brownies studded with Rolos, the chocolate-covered caramels wrapped in gold foil. They bake right into the brownies, so you get little puddles of chocolate and gooey caramel. The hardest part of this recipe is unwrapping the Rolos . . . or not eating the whole pan once the brownies are done!

MAKES 12 BROWNIES

Nonstick baking spray

2 cups all-purpose flour

⅓ cup unsweetened cocoa powder

1 teaspoon baking soda

1 teaspoon kosher salt

2 cups sugar

1¼ cups unsalted butter, melted

½ cup buttermilk

2 large eggs

2½ teaspoons vanilla extract

1½ cups Rolo caramels in milk chocolate, unwrapped

◆ Preheat the oven to 350 degrees F. Spray a 9-by-13-inch baking pan with baking spray.

◆ In a large bowl, sift the flour, cocoa powder, baking soda, and salt. Add the sugar, butter, buttermilk, eggs, and vanilla, then mix with a handheld mixer on low speed just until combined. Fold the Rolos into the batter.

◆ Pour the batter into the prepared baking pan. Bake the brownies for 20 to 25 minutes, or until a toothpick inserted into the center comes out with a few moist crumbs.

◆ Remove from the oven and let cool for at least 20 minutes before cutting. Serve and enjoy!

Salted Caramel and Chocolate Chip Cookies

Chocolate chip cookies are my ultimate fave, but I made these for my son, who is sometimes even more over the top than I am. I add caramel chips and chocolate chips to the dough, then balance out the sweetness with salt sprinkled on top. These cookies bake up soft and chewy, but if you want them more crisp, keep them in the oven a minute or two longer. I like to dip these cookies in milk (even though I don't drink milk!), or sometimes I have them with a strong cup of black coffee.

MAKES 12 COOKIES

¾ cup (1½ sticks) unsalted
  butter, softened
¼ cup butter-flavored shortening
2 medium eggs, at room temperature
1 cup packed light brown sugar
½ cup granulated sugar
2 teaspoons vanilla extract

¾ teaspoon baking soda
½ teaspoon kosher salt
2½ cups all-purpose flour
1½ cups caramel chips
1 cup semisweet chocolate chips
Vegetable oil, for greasing
2 teaspoons kosher salt

- In a large mixing bowl, using a handheld mixer with the paddle attachment, mix the butter, shortening, and eggs on medium speed. Add the brown sugar, granulated sugar, vanilla, baking soda, and kosher salt. Mix on medium speed until well combined.

- Change to the dough hook attachment. With the mixer on medium speed, gradually sprinkle in the flour and mix until everything is well combined. Add the caramel chips and chocolate chips, and mix on low speed or fold in by hand until just combined.

- Refrigerate the cookie dough for at least 2 hours.

- Preheat the oven to 350 degrees F. Lightly grease a baking sheet.

- Spoon out the dough into 12 mounds on the prepared baking sheet, spacing them 2 inches apart. Bake for 7 to 10 minutes, or until the cookies are golden brown.

- Remove the pan from the oven and transfer the cookies to a wire rack to cool. While the cookies are still warm, sprinkle the kosher salt on top and enjoy!

King Cake

It's extremely hard to find a bakery in my area that makes a good king cake, so I had to learn how to make this sweet yeasted roll myself by playing around with several different recipes. It took some time, but I finally got the cake that I was looking for: fluffy rich dough filled with pecans, brown sugar, and cinnamon. When it's Mardi Gras, I like to add colorful beads to the cake platter.

MAKES 12 SERVINGS

For the pastry:
1 cup half-and-half
¼ cup (½ stick) unsalted butter
⅔ cup warm water
2 (0.25–ounce) packets
   active dry yeast
½ cup granulated sugar, divided
2 large eggs
1½ teaspoons kosher salt
¼ teaspoon ground nutmeg
5½ cups all-purpose flour, plus more
   for dusting
Vegetable oil, for greasing

For the filling:
1 cup packed light brown sugar
⅔ cup chopped pecans
½ cup all-purpose flour
1 tablespoon ground cinnamon
½ teaspoon ground nutmeg
½ cup (1 stick) unsalted butter, melted

For the icing and decoration:
1 cup powdered sugar
1 tablespoon half-and-half
½ teaspoon vanilla extract
Green, yellow, and purple
   sparkling sugars

- First, make the pastry. In a saucepan over medium-high heat, simmer the half-and-half for 5 minutes. Remove from the heat and stir in the butter. Let cool to room temperature.

- In a large bowl, combine the warm water, yeast, and 1 tablespoon of the granulated sugar. Mix until the yeast and sugar are dissolved, then let sit until the yeast foams, about 10 minutes.

- Pour the half-and-half mixture into the yeast mixture and stir. Next, add the eggs, remaining granulated sugar, salt, and nutmeg and mix to incorporate. Gradually add the flour, 1 cup at a time, into the wet ingredients, mixing after each addition, until a dough forms.

CONTINUED

- Using a handheld mixer with the dough hook attachment, knead the dough for 10 minutes, then transfer it to a lightly oiled bowl. Cover the bowl with a kitchen towel and let rest in a warm place without any drafts for 2 hours.

- Grease a large baking sheet and set to the side.

- Meanwhile, make the filling. Combine the brown sugar, pecans, flour, cinnamon, and nutmeg, and whisk until well combined. Add the melted butter and whisk until well combined. Set to the side.

- After the 2 hours, punch the air out of the dough, then knead it on a lightly floured surface for 3 to 5 minutes. Roll out the dough into a large triangle, then slather the filling on top. Roll the dough up like a jelly roll, starting with the long side, then pull both ends of the roll together to form the dough into a circle. Pinch the ends together fully.

- Transfer the dough to the prepared baking sheet, and cover with a kitchen towel. Let the dough rise for about 1 hour.

- Preheat the oven to 375 degrees F.

- Remove the towel and place the baking sheet in the oven. Bake for 25 to 30 minutes, or until the cake is golden. Remove from the oven and let cool.

- To make the icing, in a small bowl, combine the powdered sugar, half-and-half, and vanilla. Mix until smooth.

- Drizzle the icing on the cake, then decorate with the green, yellow, and purple sugars. Let sit for at least 1 hour before serving. Enjoy!

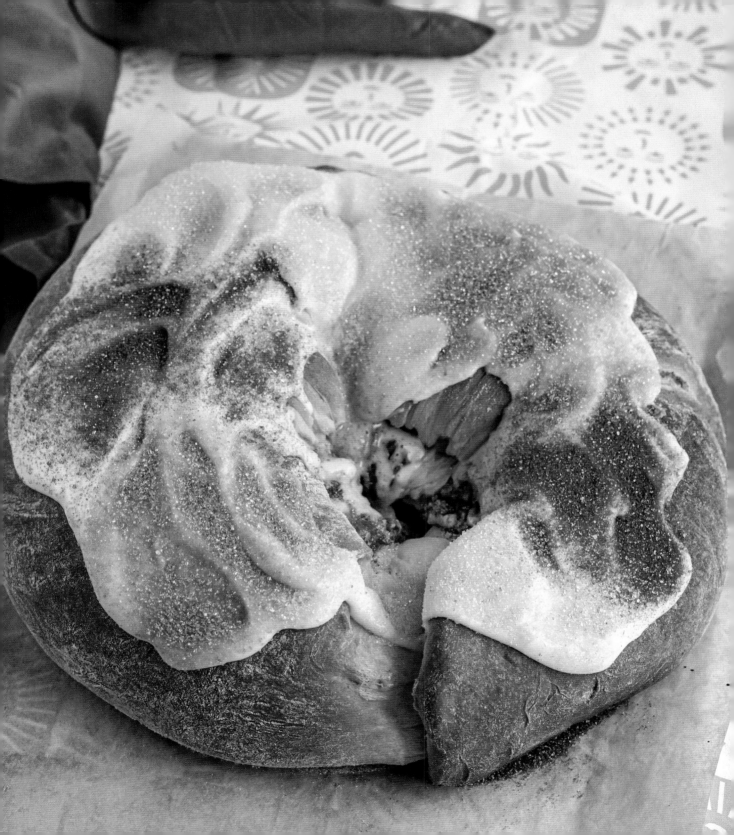

Peach Cobbler Bread Pudding

FAN FAVE!

Check your feet because this bread pudding is about to knock your socks off!

I'm very picky about my bread pudding. It must have raisins or something else to keep it interesting. When I was pregnant with my son, I craved peach cobbler like crazy. I love it so much I decided to turn it into a bread pudding. Being greedy, I then invited cinnamon rolls to this party. I use the canned kind so it's extra simple. Just bake the cinnamon rolls and let them sit overnight to dry out a bit.

I like to bring out this dessert at dinner parties. It's a real showstopper and people always ask me for the recipe. Now I can just tell them to buy this book, LOL!

MAKES 12 SERVINGS

2 (17.5-ounce) cans cinnamon
  rolls with icing
3 tablespoons salted butter, melted,
  plus more for greasing
3½ cups evaporated milk
5 medium eggs, beaten

1 cup sugar
1 tablespoon vanilla extract
2 (15-ounce) cans sliced peaches
  in heavy syrup: 1 can undrained,
  1 can drained

◆ Bake the cinnamon rolls as directed on the package but reserve and refrigerate the icing for later. Once the cinnamon rolls are done, let them sit, uncovered, overnight to dry out. (I usually do this in my turned-off oven.)

◆ Preheat the oven to 350 degrees F. Butter a 9-by-13-inch baking dish.

◆ In a large mixing bowl, whisk the milk, eggs, sugar, melted butter, and vanilla. Next, tear the cinnamon rolls apart, add them to the large mixing bowl, and stir. Let sit for about 20 minutes so the bread can soak up all the liquid.

◆ Now add the undrained can of peaches, syrup and all. Fold into the cinnamon roll mixture, then let sit for about 10 more minutes.

◆ Transfer the mixture to the prepared baking dish and smooth it out. Arrange the drained peaches on top of the bread pudding. Bake, uncovered, for about 50 minutes.

◆ Remove from the oven and let cool. Top the bread pudding with the icing that came with the cinnamon rolls. Serve warm.

Cherries and Cream Funnel Cakes

This is a take on the funnel cake that I get at the state fair every year. It wasn't until I got older that I realized it's a rip-off, because funnel cake is so easy to make! When ordering it at the fair booth, you can choose whipped cream or powdered sugar, and sometimes strawberry. I prefer cherries—I like to use fresh Rainiers in the summer, but you can use can bing or red cherries, or just cherry pie filling. Serve this cake piping hot with cherries on top, and whew, it's so good! You can use frozen cherries for the batter since it's cooked anyway.

Instead of a funnel, use a ziplock plastic bag and snip off a corner. I drizzle ½ cup batter into the oil to make the pattern. We like it simple around here!

MAKES 4 TO 6 FUNNEL CAKES

3 cups plus 2 tablespoons all-purpose flour, divided	1 teaspoon almond extract
¼ cup sugar	½ teaspoon vanilla extract
1 tablespoon baking powder	½ cup frozen cherries, diced
½ teaspoon kosher salt	4 cups vegetable oil, for deep-frying
2 cups half-and-half	Cherry pie filling, for serving
3 medium eggs	1 to 2 cups whipped cream, for serving

♦ In a large mixing bowl, combine 3 cups of the flour with the sugar, baking powder, and salt, and mix until well combined. Next, pour in the half-and-half, eggs, and both extracts. Mix until well incorporated.

♦ In a medium bowl, combine the frozen cherries with the remaining 2 tablespoons flour. Toss until the cherries are well coated. Fold them into the batter.

♦ Pour the oil into a large deep pan and heat it to 360 degrees F.

♦ Transfer the batter into a large ziplock plastic bag. Snip one corner and drizzle about ½ cup of the batter for each funnel cake into the oil. Fry, one at a time, until golden, about 4 minutes per cake. Remove the funnel cakes from the oil and set on a paper-towel-lined plate to drain.

♦ Top each funnel cake with a dollop of cherry pie filling and whipped cream and serve.

Blackberry Pie

Blackberries are popular in the Northwest. As a little kid I was always picking blackberries off a bush. You can find blackberry bushes everywhere here in Washington State. Blackberry pie happens to be my fave because the berries are always available and so, so good. The wild blackberries are considered a weed to some people because they can take over your yard, but I don't mind one bit!

If you don't have access to fresh blackberries, go ahead with frozen. I love to use cornstarch to thicken the juice—you get that glossy beautiful pie filling. The lemon zest adds a lemony flavor to the pie without too much bitterness. I like there to be crust on top and bottom. Most of my fruit pies have a double crust—a nice buttery, flaky crust. Store-bought is just fine to save time. We all know I love to cheat a little bit in the kitchen.

MAKES ONE 9-INCH PIE (ABOUT 8 SERVINGS)

For the crust:
- 1½ cups all-purpose flour, plus more for dusting
- 1 teaspoon kosher salt
- 1 cup (2 sticks) cold unsalted butter, cut into cubes, plus more for greasing
- ½ cup cold water

For the filling:
- 5 cups fresh or frozen blackberries
- 1 cup sugar
- 5 tablespoons cornstarch
- 3 tablespoons unsalted butter, melted
- 2 teaspoons vanilla extract
- 1 teaspoon grated lemon zest
- ½ teaspoon ground nutmeg

◆ First, make the crust. In a large mixing bowl, sift or whisk together the flour and salt. Next, add the cold butter, and work it in using a fork or pastry cutter. Now pour in the cold water and continue using the fork or pastry cutter to work in the ingredients until the dough is crumbly.

◆ Use your hands to work the dough into a ball. Cut it in half, and shape into 2 separate balls. Wrap each ball in plastic wrap and refrigerate for 1 hour.

◆ Preheat the oven to 375 degrees F. Lightly grease a 9-inch pie pan with butter.

CONTINUED

- Lightly flour a flat surface and remove the dough from the refrigerator. Roll out 1 of the dough balls with a rolling pin into about a 12-inch round. Place it on top of the prepared pie pan. Gently press the dough down into the pan using your fingers. Roll out the second ball of dough to the same size as the first, then set to the side.

- Next, make the filling. In a large bowl, toss together the blackberries, sugar, cornstarch, melted butter, vanilla, lemon zest, and nutmeg. Make sure everything is well combined, then pour the filling into the bottom crust.

- Top the pie with the second round of dough, and use a fork to crimp and seal the edges of the crust. Cut three ½-inch slits in the middle of the top crust.

- Place the pie in the center of the oven and bake for 45 minutes, or until the crust is golden brown. Remove the pie from the oven and let cool for at least 30 minutes before serving.

Chocolate Chess Pie

This pie is a family fave that I only make around the holidays. My son is a huge fan of buttermilk pie, but I wanted to open his eyes to other kinds of pies. Chess pie is similar to buttermilk pie, but it includes cornmeal, which adds texture and rises to the top to create a great crust. While chocolate isn't traditional for chess pie, I add it as my own delicious twist.

MAKES ONE 9-INCH PIE (8 SERVINGS)

2 cups sugar

½ cup (1 stick) unsalted butter, melted

2 teaspoons vanilla extract

5 large eggs

¼ cup whole milk

¼ cup unsweetened cocoa powder

1 tablespoon yellow cornmeal

1 tablespoon distilled white vinegar

1 (9-inch) store-bought
    pie crust, chilled

◆ Preheat the oven to 325 degrees F.

◆ In a large mixing bowl, whisk the sugar, butter, and vanilla until well combined. Add the eggs, milk, cocoa, cornmeal, and vinegar and whisk until well combined. Pour the filling into the pie crust.

◆ Bake for 1 hour and 15 minutes, or until the center of the pie is almost set. Let the pie cool on a wire rack for about 45 minutes before serving.

Chocolate Cornbread Cheesecake

My cousin Nicole and I always love to always try different things with cornbread. One day when I was at an airport, she called me up and said, "I know you're going to laugh at me, but you should make a chocolate cornbread cheesecake!" I did laugh at her but she insisted, "Trust me you should do it." Definitely random, I thought to myself, but I do love a challenge so I had to try it. I'm one of those people who says don't mess around with cornbread, but this is amazing and it works. You start with a chocolate cornbread layer on the bottom as the crust. Then there's the cheesecake layer. Followed by another layer of chocolate cornbread (surprise!). Then you pour chocolate ganache all over the top, and it becomes a delicious and unique treat that you've gotta try!

MAKES ONE 9-INCH CHEESECAKE (12 SERVINGS)

For the chocolate cornbread:
Nonstick baking spray
3 cups all-purpose flour
1¾ cups sugar
1 cup unsweetened cocoa powder
1 cup yellow cornmeal
1 tablespoon baking powder
1 teaspoon kosher salt
2½ cups buttermilk
1 cup (2 sticks) unsalted
   butter, softened
5 large eggs
½ cup vegetable oil

For the cheesecake:
16 ounces cream cheese, softened
½ cup heavy cream
¼ cup cornstarch
3 large eggs
1 tablespoon vanilla extract
1½ cups sugar
1 cup semisweet chocolate chips

For the ganache:
2 cups heavy cream
18 ounces bittersweet
   chocolate, chopped

◆ Preheat the oven to 350 degrees F. Spray three 9-inch cake pans with baking spray. Line the bottom of one of the pans with parchment paper.

◆ First, make the chocolate cornbread. In a large bowl, sift or whisk together the flour, sugar, cocoa powder, cornmeal, baking powder, and salt. Add the buttermilk, butter, eggs, and vegetable oil. Mix all the ingredients until well combined.

- Pour equal amounts of batter into the two prepared cake pans without parchment. Bake for 45 minutes, or until a toothpick inserted into the center of the cornbreads comes out clean. Remove the pans from the oven (but leave it on) and let cool completely on wire racks.

- Meanwhile, make the cheesecake filling. In a large mixing bowl, combine the cream cheese, heavy cream, and cornstarch. Using a handheld mixer, mix until light, creamy, and lump-free. Next, add the eggs, one at a time, and mix after each addition, until well incorporated. Add the vanilla, followed by the sugar. Mix until the filling is nice and smooth. Fold in the chocolate chips.

- Pour the cheesecake filling into the parchment-lined cake pan. Place the pan on a rimmed baking sheet, then pour about 1½ cups of water onto the baking sheet, *not into the cheesecake filling*. Bake for about 30 minutes, or until the cheesecake is set. Remove the pan from the oven and let cool completely on a wire rack.

- To assemble the cake, place one of the chocolate cornbreads on a cake stand or large round plate. Run a knife around the edge of the cheesecake to loosen it from the pan, and carefully turn it out onto the cornbread layer. Peel off the parchment and top the cheesecake layer with the other chocolate cornbread.

- Finally, make the ganache. In a medium saucepan over medium heat, bring the heavy cream just to a boil for only a few seconds, then remove from the heat.

- Toss the bittersweet chocolate into a large heatproof bowl, then pour in the hot cream. Whisk until nice and smooth. Let the ganache cool for a few minutes, then pour it over the cheesecake. Let the cake sit for at least 20 minutes before serving.

Strawberry Shortcake Cheesecake

Do you remember the strawberry shortcake ice cream bars from the ice cream truck? Well, that's the inspiration for this cake. I took it a step further and thought, "Wouldn't it be nice to add some cheesecake?" So I sandwich a cheesecake filling between two layers of strawberry cake, then coat the outside with crunchy strawberry shortcake crumbles—which we all know is the best part of those ice cream bars. Once I tasted the final result, I went crazy for it. Even though I'm allergic to strawberries, I'll take a Benadryl just to eat this cake. (That's why I use strawberry gelatin to flavor the cake batter, but you can use strawberry cake mix instead.)

Some people use Golden Oreos for shortcake crumbles, but I use butter ring cookies instead. They're less expensive and you don't have to scrape out any cream filling, which, in my opinion, is very disrespectful to Oreos!

This recipe is pretty time-consuming but worth it. I make it for special occasions, like Valentine's Day, and people declare it their all-time favorite cake.

MAKES ONE 9-INCH CHEESECAKE (12 SERVINGS)

For the strawberry cake:
Nonstick baking spray
1 (15.25-ounce) box white
   cake mix (see Note)
1 (6-ounce) box strawberry gelatin mix
1 cup whole milk
3 large egg whites
¼ cup vegetable oil
½ cup mashed strawberries
   (optional; see Note)

For the cheesecake:
16 ounces cream cheese,
   at room temperature
½ cup heavy cream
¼ cup cornstarch
3 large eggs
1 tablespoon vanilla extract
1½ cups granulated sugar

**For the cookie crust and
   shortcake crumble:**
2 (11.5-ounce) packages butter ring
   cookies, divided (see Note)
½ cup (1 stick) unsalted butter, divided
2 tablespoons ice water, divided
1 (6-ounce) box strawberry gelatin mix
3 drops red food coloring

For the frosting:
8 ounces cream cheese, at room
   temperature
½ cup (1 stick) unsalted
   butter, softened
½ cup heavy cream
1 tablespoon vanilla extract
2¼ cups powdered sugar

CONTINUED

FOR THE STRAWBERRY CAKE:

* Preheat the oven to 350 degrees F. Spray two 9-inch cake pans with baking spray.

* Put the cake mix into a large mixing bowl and whisk to remove any lumps. Next, sprinkle in the gelatin mix and whisk to incorporate.

* Add the milk, egg whites, and oil. Using a handheld mixer, mix on low speed until the batter is smooth and lump-free. If you're adding the mashed strawberries, fold them in now.

* Pour equal amounts of batter into the prepared cake pans, filling each one about three-fourths full. Bake for about 20 minutes, or until a toothpick inserted into the center comes out with a few moist crumbs.

* Remove the pans from the oven, let sit for 5 minutes, then remove the cakes from the pans and transfer them to a wire rack to cool completely. Leave the oven on.

FOR THE CHEESECAKE:

* Spray a 9-inch cake pan with baking spray and line the bottom with parchment paper. Place the pan on a rimmed baking sheet, then pour about 1½ cups of water onto the baking sheet, *not into the cake pan.*

* In a large mixing bowl, combine the cream cheese, heavy cream, and cornstarch. Using a handheld mixer, mix on medium speed until light, creamy, and lump-free. Next, add the eggs, one at a time, and mix after each addition, until well incorporated. Add the vanilla, followed by the sugar. Mix until the filling is nice and smooth.

* Pour 3 cups of the cheesecake filling into the prepared cake pan. Reserve the remaining filling for the crust.

* Bake at 350 degrees F for about 30 minutes, or until the cheesecake is set. Remove the pan from the oven and let cool completely on a wire rack. Leave the oven on.

FOR THE COOKIE CRUST AND SHORTCAKE CRUMBLE:

* Spray a 9-inch springform pan with baking spray.

* In a food processor, combine 15 of the butter cookies with ¼ cup of the butter and 1 tablespoon of the ice water. Pulse until the mixture resembles cookie dough. Transfer the mixture to the prepared pan and press it into the bottom and about ¼ inch up the sides.

* Bake the cookie crust at 350 degrees F for 15 minutes. Remove the pan from the oven and let cool completely on a wire rack. Leave the oven on.

* Pour the reserved cheesecake filling into the cookie crust and smooth out the top. Bake for 30 to 35 minutes, or until the cheesecake is set. Remove the pan from the

oven and let cool completely on a wire rack. Once cool, run a knife around the edge of the pan, release the springform ring, and carefully transfer the cheesecake with crust onto a cake stand or large round plate. Leave the oven on.

◆ Meanwhile, line a rimmed baking sheet with aluminum foil.

◆ In the food processor, combine the remaining butter cookies with the remaining ¼ cup butter and 1 tablespoon ice water. Pulse until large crumbs form. Remove half of the crumbs from the food processor and set to the side.

◆ Add the gelatin mix and food coloring to the food processor. Pulse about 5 times, or until the crumbs are red. Spread the red crumbs on the prepared baking sheet, followed by the reserved white crumbs.

◆ Bake for 10 minutes, or until the crumbs are crisp. Remove the baking sheet from the oven and let cool on a wire rack. Using your fingers, break the mixture apart into crumbles. Turn off the oven.

FOR THE FROSTING:

◆ In a large mixing bowl, combine the cream cheese and butter. Using a handheld mixer, mix on medium speed until well incorporated. Add the heavy cream and vanilla and mix until well combined. Sprinkle in the powdered sugar and mix until the frosting is smooth and lump-free.

TO ASSEMBLE THE CAKE:

◆ Top the cheesecake with crust on the cake stand with one of the strawberry cakes, then the crustless cheesecake, and finally, the second strawberry cake.

◆ Frost the top and sides of the entire cake. Sprinkle with the shortcake crumbs and pat onto the sides all around the cake. Let the cake sit for about 20 minutes before cutting into it.

NOTES:

For the cake mix, make sure that you follow the instructions on the cake box, but replace the water with whole milk.

I'm allergic to strawberries, so I don't add the mashed strawberries to my cake. It still comes out fine, but feel free to add them to yours. You can also decorate the top of the cake with fresh strawberries!

The butter ring cookies that I use are Lil' Dutch Maid, but you can substitute Golden Oreos (minus the cream filling).

Caramel Cake

FAN FAVE!

People have been asking me to make this cake for years, but I needed to simplify it. Many caramel cakes take a lot of time and steps, but I love a great cake with simple shortcuts. I chose a classic yellow cake, and I wanted the caramel frosting to be easy as well. For this recipe, I've come up with one of the simplest caramel frostings I've ever made! You want it light, airy, and fluffy. If you don't mix it for twenty minutes, it will harden, and you won't get the results you are looking for. This icing needs to be creamy and spreadable, so let your stand mixer help out. I don't recommend using a whisk. They had that kinda time back in the day, but we don't have time for that these days!

MAKES ONE 9-INCH TWO-LAYER CAKE (12 SERVINGS)

For the cake:

1 cup (2 sticks) unsalted butter, softened, plus more for greasing

3 cups cake flour, plus more for dusting

2 cups sugar

6 medium eggs

1 tablespoon vanilla extract

4 teaspoons baking powder

½ teaspoon kosher salt

1 cup buttermilk

For the caramel frosting:

2¾ cups sugar, divided

1 cup heavy cream

2 tablespoons all-purpose flour

¾ cup (1½ sticks) salted butter

1 tablespoon vanilla extract

◆ Preheat the oven to 350 degrees F. Butter and flour two 9-inch cake pans.

◆ To make the cake, in a large mixing bowl, cream together the butter, sugar, eggs, and vanilla.

◆ In a medium bowl, sift or whisk together the flour, baking powder, and salt.

◆ While mixing on low speed, alternate adding the dry ingredients and buttermilk to the bowl with the creamed butter until the batter is nice and smooth.

◆ Pour the batter into the prepared cake pans. Bake for 25 to 30 minutes, or until a toothpick inserted into the center comes out with a few moist crumbs. Remove the pans from the oven and carefully remove the cakes from the pans, then let them cool completely on a wire rack.

- To make the frosting, heat ¼ cup of the sugar in a saucepan or pot over medium heat. Let the sugar melt and turn brown, 3 to 5 minutes.

- Meanwhile, in a separate large pot, combine the remaining 2½ cups sugar with the cream and flour. Stir well and bring to a boil.

- Add 3 tablespoons of the cream mixture to the melted sugar and stir, then pour this mixture into the pot with the cream mixture and stir it in. Cook over medium heat for 10 to 15 minutes.

- Next, add the butter and stir until it is well incorporated. Remove the pot from the heat and add the vanilla.

- Pour the caramel into a stand mixer bowl or a use a handheld mixer with a heat-resistant mixing bowl. Mix for 20 minutes on medium speed, then let sit for about 15 minutes.

- Place three-fourths of the caramel frosting in a separate bowl, cover, and place in the freezer for 10 minutes.

- To assemble the cake, transfer one of the cake rounds to a large round plate or cake stand. Pour some of the remaining one-fourth caramel frosting on top of the cake, then top with the second cake. Beware that the caramel will be really slippery, so don't overdo the filling.

- Remove the caramel frosting from the freezer and stir. Frost the cake on all sides, then let sit for at least 20 minutes before serving.

Coconut Cake

I made this cake in one of my first videos that went viral. Big food blogs featured it, and everyone absolutely went crazy and loved the recipe. I'm a coconut fiend, so I bump up the flavor even more with coconut extract. To go beyond, use coconut cream instead of milk in the batter. The cake's texture is light and fluffy. It's also uncomplicated but still impressive enough for Easter, Thanksgiving, or Christmas. This will become a staple at your celebration tables!

MAKES ONE 9-INCH TWO-LAYER CAKE (12 SERVINGS)

For the cake:
1½ cups (3 sticks) unsalted butter, softened, plus more for greasing
2½ cups cake flour, plus more for dusting
1 tablespoon baking powder
1 teaspoon kosher salt
5 large egg whites
2 cups granulated sugar
2 teaspoons coconut extract
1½ teaspoons vanilla extract
¾ cup whole milk or coconut cream

For the topping and frosting:
1½ cups sweetened shredded coconut
8 ounces cream cheese, softened
½ cup (1 stick) unsalted butter, softened
½ cup heavy cream
5 cups powdered sugar
1½ teaspoons vanilla extract

- Preheat the oven to 350 degrees F. Grease and lightly flour two 9-inch round cake pans.

- First, make the cake. In a large mixing bowl, sift or whisk the flour, baking powder, and salt. Set aside.

- In a separate large bowl, combine the butter, egg whites, and granulated sugar. Using a handheld mixer, mix on medium speed until creamy, 2 to 3 minutes. Add both extracts and mix until incorporated. Then add the milk and mix until incorporated.

- Add the wet ingredients to the dry ingredients and mix on low speed just until combined. Do not overmix. Divide the batter evenly among the prepared cake pans.

CONTINUED

◆ Bake on the same rack for 25 to 30 minutes, or until a toothpick inserted into the center of each cake comes out clean. Remove the pans from the oven but leave the oven on.

◆ Let the cakes cool in the pans for a few minutes, then carefully remove them to cool completely on wire racks.

◆ Meanwhile, prepare the topping: spread the shredded coconut on a rimmed baking sheet and bake until just lightly toasted, 3 to 5 minutes, watching carefully so it doesn't burn.

◆ To make the frosting, combine the cream cheese and butter in a large mixing bowl. Using a handheld mixer, mix on medium-low speed until incorporated, 3 to 4 minutes. Add the cream and mix until well combined. Add the powdered sugar and vanilla and mix on medium speed until smooth and creamy.

◆ To assemble the cake, spread some of the frosting on top of one cake round. Stack the second cake on top. Transfer the stacked cake to a cake plate or stand. Spread frosting all around the sides and top of the cake. Sprinkle the toasted coconut over the top and sides, then serve.

Moist 7UP Cake

FAN FAVE!

When I first got with my husband, he said his favorite dessert was 7UP cake. In the heat of the moment, I lied and said I could make it even though I had never attempted one before. To be honest, I had never heard of 7UP cake! We never called it that in my household. For many years, I just thought it was lemon cake.

I finally admitted to never making it before. He took the lie like a champ and put me on the phone with his grandma, who he said made the best 7UP cake, to get her advice. She said, "You have to use name-brand everything. Swift cake flour, C&H sugar, real 7UP . . . everything." She gave me a lot of pointers to make the best cake, and that was my last conversation with her before she passed.

My recipe was inspired by her, even though I never got to try hers myself. I don't know if mine held a match to her prized cake, but my husband loves it. But I'll never ask him if it's as good as his grandma's!

MAKES 16 SERVINGS

For the cake:
Nonstick baking spray (optional)
3 cups all-purpose flour
3 cups granulated sugar
½ teaspoon kosher salt
5 large eggs
1 cup (2 sticks) unsalted
    butter, softened

1 cup 7UP
1 tablespoon vanilla extract

For the icing or glaze:
1 cup powdered sugar (for an icing) or
    granulated sugar (for a glaze)
¼ cup 7UP

◆ Preheat the oven to 325 degrees F. Set out a Bundt pan—if it isn't nonstick, grease it with baking spray.

◆ In a large mixing bowl, whisk together the flour, granulated sugar, and salt until it is lump-free and well combined.

◆ In a medium mixing bowl, whisk the eggs until the color is completely yellow. Pour the eggs into the flour mixture and add the butter. Using a handheld mixer, mix on medium speed until everything is completely incorporated. Then pour in the 7UP and vanilla and mix on medium speed until the batter is smooth.

CONTINUED

- Pour the batter into the prepared Bundt pan. Let the batter sit in the pan for 3 minutes.

- Bake for 65 minutes, or until a toothpick inserted near the center of the cake comes out clean. Remove from the oven, let sit for 5 minutes, then carefully invert the cake onto a wire rack and remove the pan. Let the cake cool completely.

- To make the icing or glaze, in a medium mixing bowl, combine the powdered or granulated sugar and 7UP and whisk until the sugar dissolves. Spoon the icing over the cooled cake and let it set for at least 20 minutes before serving.

The Ultimate Carrot Cake

If you were to ask me what my favorite cake was, it'd be tough but I would have to say either carrot cake or banana cake. This carrot cake mimics one from a local grocery store that's called the colossal carrot cake. Some carrot cakes are just a spice cake with carrots for moisture, but I like my carrot cake fully loaded with lots of carrots, raisins, crushed pineapple, and coconut. If my carrot cake doesn't have coconut, I don't want it! If you don't care for coconut or chopped nuts, simply leave them out, but the coconut makes it for me. I mince the raisins so they can distribute evenly—I get upset if I see that someone else has more raisins in their slice than mine! This is truly the ultimate carrot cake—and don't forget that cream cheese icing. You will never bake a different carrot cake recipe again!

MAKES ONE 9-INCH TWO-LAYER CAKE (12 SERVINGS)

For the cake:
¾ cup vegetable oil, plus more
    for greasing
2 cups all-purpose flour,
    plus more for dusting
1½ cups granulated sugar
¾ cup buttermilk
3 large eggs
1 tablespoon baking powder
1 tablespoon ground cinnamon
¾ teaspoon ground nutmeg
½ teaspoon kosher salt
2 cups shredded carrots

1 cup unsweetened applesauce
½ cup raisins, minced
⅓ cup crushed pineapple, drained
¼ cup sweetened shredded coconut
1 tablespoon vanilla extract

For the cream cheese frosting:
8 ounces cream cheese, softened
½ cup (1 stick) unsalted
    butter, softened
4½ cups powdered sugar
2 teaspoons vanilla extract

◆ Preheat the oven to 350 degrees F. Lightly grease and flour two 9-inch cake pans.

◆ In a large mixing bowl, using a handheld mixer, mix the oil, granulated sugar, buttermilk, and eggs until well combined.

◆ In a medium mixing bowl, sift or whisk together the flour, baking powder, cinnamon, nutmeg, and salt. Slowly add the dry ingredients to the wet ingredients and mix well.

◆ In another medium bowl, stir together the carrots, applesauce, raisins, pineapple, shredded coconut, and vanilla. Fold everything into the batter.

- Divide the batter evenly among the prepared pans. Bake on the same rack for 30 to 40 minutes, or until a toothpick inserted into the center of each cake comes out clean. Let the cakes cool completely in the pans before frosting.

- Meanwhile, make the frosting. In a large mixing bowl, using a handheld mixer, mix the cream cheese and butter on medium speed until light and fluffy, 2 to 3 minutes. Add the powdered sugar and vanilla, then mix on medium speed until smooth and creamy.

- To assemble the cake, spread some of the frosting on top of one of the cake rounds. Top with the second cake. Transfer the stacked cake to a cake plate or stand. Frost the cake on all sides, then let sit for at least 30 minutes before serving.

Three-Layer Key Lime Cake with Key Lime Buttercream Frosting

Before I started making this as a three-layer cake, I made it as a pound cake with icing. But by turning it into a layer cake, I could indulge in more sweets—meaning the frosting! Each layer is the same: zesty cake with key lime buttercream frosting in between and all over. This happy, citrusy cake is great for any birthday celebration or festive gathering.

Some people have a hard time finding key lime, so you can substitute regular lime if needed. Never heard of key limes? Well, they are generally very small and have a great tangy lime flavor. I love using cake flour for this recipe; its lighter texture—cornstarch is added to the flour—makes a difference. But don't worry if you don't have any, just go ahead with all-purpose.

MAKES ONE 9-INCH THREE-LAYER CAKE (12 SERVINGS)

For the cake:
Nonstick baking spray
4 cups cake flour
2 teaspoons baking powder
1 teaspoon kosher salt
2 cups granulated sugar
2 cups (4 sticks) unsalted
    butter, softened
4 medium eggs, at room temperature
½ cup freshly squeezed key lime juice
1 tablespoon grated key lime zest

2½ teaspoons vanilla extract
1 cup half-and-half

For the buttercream frosting:
16 ounces cream cheese, softened
1 cup (2 sticks) unsalted butter,
    softened
10 cups powdered sugar
¼ cup freshly squeezed key lime juice
1 tablespoon vanilla extract

◆ Preheat the oven to 350 degrees F. Spray a deep 9-inch round cake pan with baking spray.

◆ In a medium mixing bowl, sift or whisk together the flour, baking powder, and salt until well combined.

- In a large mixing bowl, using a handheld mixer, cream the granulated sugar and butter together on medium speed until light and fluffy. Then add 1 egg at a time, mixing after each addition, until everything is nice and creamy. Add the key lime juice and zest and the vanilla, and mix to combine.

- Alternate adding the dry ingredients and half-and-half to the wet ingredients, mixing after each addition, until the batter is nice and smooth. Let it sit for a few minutes, then pour the batter into the prepared cake pan.

- Bake for 30 to 35 minutes, or until a wooden skewer inserted in the center of the cake comes out clean. Remove the pan from the oven and set on a wire rack to let the cake cool.

- Meanwhile, make the frosting. In a large mixing bowl, using a handheld mixer, mix the cream cheese and butter on medium speed until well combined. Gradually add the powdered sugar while mixing on low speed. Next, pour in the key lime juice and vanilla. Mix until the frosting is nice and creamy. Place in the refrigerator for 30 minutes.

- Once the cake is almost fully cooled, carefully remove it from the pan. Cut the cake horizontally into three even layers.

- Place the bottom cake layer on a large round plate or cake stand. Top with a thin layer of frosting, then another layer of cake. Add another thin layer of frosting, then top with the final cake layer. Frost the top and sides of the entire cake. Enjoy!

Sippin' Tipsy

Easy Strawberry Lemonade	224
Pink Moscato Lemonade	227
Pineapple Hennyrita	228
Frozen Green Sweet Tea	229
Grown Folks Peach Sweet Tea	230
Boss Lady Cocktail	232
Cherry Mojito	233
Island Girl Cocktail	234

Easy Strawberry Lemonade

FAN FAVE!

Here's another recipe I can't have due to my strawberry allergy, but I make it for others because they love it. (I use cherries or blackberries for myself.) This lemonade is a refreshing drink for brunch and wholesome enough for kids and Bible study groups—Southern households always have to have a beverage for Bible study. For a grown-up version, you can add a little somethin' somethin', but don't let the church folks know.

MAKES 8 SERVINGS

For the simple syrup:
1 cup water
1 cup sugar

For the lemonade:
½ pound fresh strawberries, sliced,
    plus more for garnish
1 cup freshly squeezed lemon juice
    (from 5 to 6 large lemons)
6 cups cold water
Lemon slices, for garnish (optional)

◆ To make the simple syrup, in a medium saucepan over medium heat, bring the water to a low boil. Add the sugar and whisk until it dissolves. Remove from the heat and let the syrup cool.

◆ To make the lemonade, combine the strawberries and lemon juice in a blender. Blend until smooth, then transfer to a large pitcher. Add the cold water and simple syrup, and stir until everything is well combined.

◆ Put the lemon and strawberry slices into the pitcher, reserving some for the glasses, if desired. Pour the lemonade into tall glasses over ice.

Pink Moscato Lemonade

FAN FAVE!

Confession: I am a moscato addict. I make any excuse to have it any time of day. I would sneak it into juice or lemonade, and it turns out my friends love it too! So that's how my pink moscato lemonade became the most requested drink . . . for girls' day or barbecues or really any gathering. They all ask, "Can you bring your pink moscato lemonade, please?" My answer is always yes because I get to enjoy it too.

Since it will be combined with tart fresh lemon juice, the type of moscato you use has to be sweet. Don't use any of that super dry stuff!

MAKES 8 SERVINGS

For the simple syrup:
1 cup water
1 cup sugar

For the lemonade:
1 (750-milliliter bottle) pink moscato, chilled
1 cup freshly squeezed lemon juice (from 5 to 6 large lemons)
Lemon slices, for garnish (optional)

◆ To make the simple syrup, in a medium saucepan over medium heat, bring the water to a low boil. Add the sugar and whisk until it dissolves. Remove from the heat and let the syrup cool.

◆ To make the lemonade, pour the moscato, lemon juice, and simple syrup into a large pitcher and stir until well combined. Refrigerate until ready to serve.

◆ Pour the lemonade over ice into tall glasses and garnish with lemon slices before serving.

Pineapple Hennyrita

I love Hennessy and I love margaritas. But margaritas can sometimes be on the weaker side, so I decided to make mine stronger with Hennessy. Serve this drink in a pineapple bowl: scoop out the flesh and toss it in a blender until it's nice and airy and creamy, then add the liquor. But don't stop there! Place small Henny bottles upside down in the drink and you've got a showstopper. I saw that in Vegas. Pour shots into the pineapple to refill it: it's fun and feels like you're getting away with something! This drink is not for the weak, so pass it on to your boss friends! Definitely whip this up for girls' night or a bachelorette party, and let loose.

MAKES 2 SERVINGS

1 large pineapple	2 to 3 ounces Hennessy
3 cups ice cubes	Several 50-milliliter Hennessy
4 to 5 ounces tequila	minibottles (optional)
2 to 3 ounces triple sec	Lime wedges, for garnish
2 to 3 ounces margarita mix	Pineapple wedges, for garnish

◆ Slice the top off of the pineapple, then scoop out the flesh and transfer it to a blender. Blend until nice and creamy.

◆ Add the ice, tequila, triple sec, margarita mix, and Hennessy. Blend everything until it's slushy.

◆ Pour the slushy goodness into the pineapple bowl (or 2 glasses). Open a Hennessy minibottle or two, and place it upside down in the pineapple.

◆ Garnish with lime and pineapple wedges. Drink responsibly!

Frozen Green Sweet Tea

I like this recipe because it's another ice tea but uses green tea, which I feel is underappreciated. It's green and floral and a bit lighter than the traditional black or English teas. I sweeten this with honey instead of adding an extra step to make simple syrup. Essentially you are making a concentrated tea to whirl up with ice in the blender for the perfect tea slushie. I love it especially in the summertime.

MAKES 8 SERVINGS	
4 cups water	¼ cup freshly squeezed lemon juice
2 gallon-size green tea bags	(from 1 to 2 large lemons)
¾ cup honey	4 cups crushed ice

- In a medium saucepan, bring the water to a boil, then remove from the heat. Add the tea bags and let steep for 20 minutes. Discard the tea bags. Add the honey and lemon juice, and stir until well incorporated.

- Pour the tea into a large freezer bag and seal it tightly. Freeze for 1 hour.

- In a blender, combine the frozen tea with the crushed ice. Blend until well blended and serve in tall glasses.

Grown Folks Peach Sweet Tea

Whenever we had a cookout, there'd always be two kinds of drinks: one for the kids and the other for "grown folks." All the kids knew there was something special in that forbidden grown folks' drink.

Now that I'm of age, I can make my own grown folks' drink for the cookout. I like to make a big batch of ice tea sweetened with homemade peach syrup and spike it with Peach Crown Royal. This is a seasonal Canadian whisky that's only available during the summer, so when it comes out, I stock up on four bottles for the year.

If you can't find Peach Crown Royal, there's a knockoff version called Ensign Red Peach, which is less expensive and will still do the trick.

MAKES 8 SERVINGS

For the peach syrup:	For the sweet tea:
4½ cups frozen sliced peaches	5½ cups water
2 cups water	4 quart-size black tea bags
2 cups sugar	2 cups Peach Crown Royal whisky

◆ To make the peach syrup, in a large saucepan, combine the peaches with the water and sugar. Bring to a simmer over medium heat and cook until the peaches soften, about 15 minutes. Using a potato masher, mash the peaches, then cook for about 10 more minutes. Strain the peach mixture, toss the peach pieces, and set the syrup aside.

◆ Meanwhile, make the tea. In a large pot, bring the water to a boil, then remove from the heat. Add the tea bags to the water and let steep for 20 minutes. Discard the tea bags. Add the Peach Crown Royal and peach syrup to the pot and stir to incorporate.

◆ Transfer the sweet tea to a pitcher and refrigerate until it's nice and cold, about 2 hours.

◆ Fill 8 tall glasses with ice, then pour in the tea. Serve and enjoy!

Boss Lady Cocktail

Guess what? I like dark liquor! One of my favorites happens to be Hennessy. And I like Disaronno because it goes great with Hennessy and Cherry Coke. And yes, I like trap music too! After a long day running several businesses, sometimes I just want to take the edge off, and that's exactly what I do with my Boss Lady Cocktail. I turn on some Nicki Minaj and grab all the ingredients. I simply add everything in the shaker, then pour it over ice. I'm a little extra, so I add cherries and a lime wedge as well, but that part is completely optional.

MAKES 1 DRINK

6 ounces Cherry Coke	Juice from ¼ small lime
2 to 3 ounces Disaronno	2 cherries, for garnish
1 to 2 ounces Hennessy	Lime wedge, for garnish

◆ In a cocktail shaker, combine the Cherry Coke, Disaronno, Hennessy, and lime juice, and shake two or three times.

◆ Pour into a rocks glass filled with ice and toss in the cherries and lime wedge.

Cherry Mojito

A regular mojito is good but adding cherries or berries makes it much, much better. I usually use frozen cherries because they keep the drink cold, so you don't need to water it down with as much ice. But fresh cherries work as well. I like to serve this drink for social events, little get-togethers, girls' nights, and barbecues! It instantly brings a little fun and class to your cocktail bar setup. Your guests will get a kick out of making this while you get the snacks out—I like to post the recipe next to the ingredients, and then tell my friends and family to help themselves.

MAKES 1 DRINK

10 frozen cherries, mashed or blended
6 fresh mint leaves, roughly chopped
½ cup ice
1 tablespoon honey
3 tablespoons white rum

3 tablespoons freshly
  squeezed lime juice
2 tablespoons club soda, chilled
2 lime slices, for garnish

◆ Combine the cherries, mint, and ice in a tall glass. Drizzle in the honey, then add the rum, lime juice, and club soda. Stir everything together, then garnish with the lime slices.

Island Girl Cocktail

One time I didn't have all of the ingredients to make a "fast piña colada"—you know, with all the fancy syrups—but I was really craving that kind of drink. I had to get creative and use what I had on hand. This is the super soulful way to make a drink. *Use what you have on hand.* That's when I came up with the Island Girl Cocktail. I had some leftover frozen mangoes from a smoothie and some leftover cream of coconut from a recipe I made the day before. I mixed them with rum (two kinds, to be exact!), pineapple juice, and crushed ice, and *baby*, it was love after first, second, and third sip!

MAKES 1 DRINK

½ cup frozen mango cubes	3 to 4 ounces coconut rum
½ cup pineapple juice	1 to 2 ounces spiced rum
½ cup crushed ice	2 tablespoons cream of coconut

◆ Combine all the ingredients in a blender and blend until well combined. Pour into a tall glass and enjoy!

ACKNOWLEDGMENTS

First and foremost, I want to thank God for guiding me through this journey and never giving up on me. All glory and praises to my Lord, because without him I would not be here.

A very special thanks to Danielle and Michael Kartes! Thank you for stepping up when needed. You're amazing, and I truly appreciate ya'll! I'd also like to thank the wonderful team at Sasquatch Books.

INDEX

Note: Page numbers in *italic* refer to photographs.

A

appetizers, 53–83
Apple Fritter Bread, 101–102, *103*
Apples, Southern Fried Cinnamon, 34
Artichoke Au Gratin Dip, Turnip Greens and, *54*, 55
author's story, 3–7

B

bacon
  Bacon-Wrapped Stuffed Chicken Thighs, 134, *135*
  Bacon-Wrapped Stuffed Jalapeños, *64*, 65
  Creamed Spinach with Bacon, 166
  Creole Loaded Potato Skins, 61–62, *63*
  Meat Lover's Quiche, 42, *43*
  Not Yo' Mama's Bacon Caesar Salad, 108, *109*
  Roasted Parsnips with Bacon, 172
  Savory Monkey Bread, *90*, 91
  Soulful Cabbage and Collard Greens, 164, *165*
  Three-Cheese, Bacon, and Herb Biscuits, 92, *93*
  Turnip Greens and Artichoke Au Gratin Dip, *54*, 55
  Ultimate Breakfast Sandwich, 35
baking essentials, 14–16
beans
  Country Steak Chili, 120, *121*
  dried, tips for prepping, 19
  White Beans and Sausage, *178*, 179

beef
  Country Steak Chili, 120, *121*
  Easy Slow Cooker Short Ribs, *150*, 151
  Jamaican Oxtails, 152, *153*
  Philly Cheesesteak Lasagna, 147–148, *149*
  Southern Meat Pies with Creole Chimichurri, 82–83, *83*
  Steak and Cheese Omelette, 41
Beignets, Real Deal, 104–105, *105*
beverages, 223–235
biscuits
  Cherry Pie Biscuits, 96, *97*
  Garlicky Cheese Drop Biscuits, 94
  Red Velvet Biscuits, 95
  Three-Cheese, Bacon, and Herb Biscuits, 92, *93*
Blackberry Pie, 199–200, *201*
Blackberry-Glazed Ribs, 158–159, *159*
Boss Lady Cocktail, 232
Boudin Balls, 80–81
Bread Pudding, Peach Cobbler, *196*, 197
breads, 85–105
breakfast, 29–51
Broccoli Casserole, Southern, 167
Brownies, Rolo, *190*, 191
Butter, Seasoned, 139
Butter Pecan Scones, *98*, 99

C

Cabbage and Collard Greens, Soulful, 164, *165*
cakes
  Caramel Cake, 210–211
  Cherries and Cream Funnel Cakes, 198
  Chocolate Cornbread Cheesecake, 204–205
  Coconut Cake, *212*, 213–214

King Cake, 193–194, *195*

Moist 7UP Cake, 215–216, *217*

Strawberry Shortcake Cheesecake, *206*, 207–209

Three-Layer Key Lime Cake with Key Lime Buttercream Frosting, 220–221

Ultimate Carrot Cake, The, 218–219, *219*

Caramel Cake, 210–211

Carrot Cake, The Ultimate, 218–219, *219*

casseroles

Cheddar, Ham, and Grits Casserole, *50*, 51

Corn Pudding Casserole, 176

Five-Cheese Hash Brown Casserole, 47

Southern Baked Macaroni and Cheese Casserole, 182–183

Southern Broccoli Casserole, 167

Catfish and Oyster Po'boys, Spicy, 118–119

cheese

Cheddar, Ham, and Grits Casserole, *50*, 51

Five-Cheese Hash Brown Casserole, 47

Garlicky Cheese Drop Biscuits, 94

Philly Cheesesteak Lasagna, 147–148, *149*

Savory Monkey Bread, *90*, 91

Southern Baked Macaroni and Cheese Casserole, 182–183

Steak and Cheese Omelette, 41

Stuffed Hash Browns, 48, *49*

Three-Cheese, Bacon, and Herb Biscuits, *92*, *93*

Turnip Greens and Artichoke Au Gratin Dip, *54*, 55

Voodoo Dip, 56, *57*

Cheesecake, Chocolate Cornbread, 204–205

Cheesecake, Strawberry Shortcake, *206*, 207–209

Cherries and Cream Funnel Cakes, 198

Cherry Mojito, 233

Cherry Pie Biscuits, *96*, *97*

Chess Pie, Chocolate, *202*, 203

chicken. *See* poultry

Chili, Country Steak, 120, *121*

Chili Sauce, Sweet, 72, *73*

Chimichurri, Creole, 82, *83*

Cobbler Bread Pudding, Peach, *196*, 197

Cocktail Sauce, 67–68, *69*

cocktails, 223–235

Coconut Cake, *212*, 213–214

collard greens. *See* greens

cookies

Better-Than-Sex Cookies, 188, *189*

Salted Caramel and Chocolate Chip Cookies, 192

corn

Corn Pudding Casserole, 176

Creole Street Corn, 173

Fresh Creamed Corn, *174*, 175

Seafood Boil with Creole Garlic Sauce, *130*, 131–132

cornbread

Chocolate Cornbread Cheesecake, 204–205

Corn Pudding Casserole, 176

Cracklin' Cornbread, 88–89, *89*

Hot-Water Cornbread, 86, *87*

Cornish Game Hens, Deep-Fried, *144*, 145–146

crabmeat

Creole Crab Cakes with Sweet Chili Sauce, 72, *73*

Poached Garlic Crab Legs, 74

Seafood Boil with Creole Garlic Sauce, *130*, 131–132

Seafood Lasagna, 128–129

Cracklin' Cornbread, 88–89, *89*

crawfish, in Mardi Gras Pasta Salad, 111

D

desserts, 185–221

dips

Turnip Greens and Artichoke Au Gratin Dip, *54*, 55

Voodoo Dip, 56, *57*

Dressing, Collard Green and Smoked Turkey, 168–169

drinks, 223–235

Dumplings, Best Damn Chicken and, 136–137, *137*

E

eggs
  Cousin Rosie's Macaroni Salad, 110
  Egg, Sausage, and Potato Scramble, 36, *37*
  Five-Cheese Hash Brown Casserole, 47
  Meat Lover's Quiche, 42, *43*
  Soulful Breakfast Enchiladas, *38*, 39–40
  Steak and Cheese Omelette, 41
  Stuffed Hash Browns, 48, *49*
  Ultimate Breakfast Sandwich, 35
Enchiladas, Soulful Breakfast, *38*, 39–40

F

fan favorites
  Bacon-Wrapped Stuffed Jalapeños, *64*, 65
  Caramel Cake, 210–211
  Coconut Cake, *212*, 213–214
  Collard Green and Smoked Turkey Dressing, 168–169
  Corn Pudding Casserole, 176
  Cousin Rosie's Macaroni Salad, 110
  Deep-Fried Cornish Game Hens, *144*, 145–146
  Easy Slow Cooker Short Ribs, *150*, 151
  Easy Smoked Whole Turkey, *138*, 139–140
  Easy Strawberry Lemonade, 224, *225*
  Egg, Sausage, and Potato Scramble, 36, *37*
  Fresh Creamed Corn, *174*, 175
  Hot-Water Cornbread, 86, *87*
  Moist 7UP Cake, 215–216, *217*
  Peach Cobbler Bread Pudding, *196*, 197
  Philly Cheesesteak Lasagna, 147–148, *149*
  Pink Moscato Lemonade, *226*, 227
  Red Velvet Biscuits, 95
  Seafood Boil with Creole Garlic Sauce, *130*, 131–132
  Slow Cooker Neck Bones and Potatoes, *160*, 161
  Slow Cooker Smothered Turkey Wings, 141–142, *143*
  Soulful Cabbage and Collard Greens, 164, *165*

  Southern Baked Macaroni and Cheese Casserole, 182–183
  Strawberry Shortcake Cheesecake, *206*, 207–209
  Waffle Fried Chicken, *44*, 45–46
fish
  Blackened Salmon, *126*, 127
  Fried Salmon Bites, *70*, 71
  Fried Tilapia Sandwiches, 114, *115*
  Spicy Catfish and Oyster Po'boys, 118–119
French Toast, Cinnamon Toast Crunch, *32*, 33
Funnel Cakes, Cherries and Cream, 198

G

Garlic Sauce, Creole, *130*, 131–132
greens
  basic preparation tips, 21
  Collard Green and Smoked Turkey Dressing, 168–169
  Creamed Spinach with Bacon, 166
  Soulful Cabbage and Collard Greens, 164, *165*
  Turnip Greens and Artichoke Au Gratin Dip, *54*, 55
Grits Casserole, Cheddar, Ham, and, *50*, 51

H

ham
  Cheddar, Ham, and Grits Casserole, *50*, 51
  Meat Lover's Quiche, 42, *43*
  Muffuletta, *116*, 117
  Ultimate Breakfast Sandwich, 35
hash browns
  Five-Cheese Hash Brown Casserole, 47
  Stuffed Hash Browns, 48, *49*
Hennyrita, Pineapple, 228
herbs and spices, 10–14, *12*
Hummingbird Bread, 100

I

ingredients, essential, 9–21
Island Girl Cocktail, 234, *235*

J

Jalapeños, Bacon-Wrapped Stuffed, *64*, 65

K

Key Lime Cake with Key Lime Buttercream
    Frosting, Three-Layer, 220–221
King Cake, 193–194, *195*
kitchen tools, 23–27

L

lamb
    Cajun-Style Leg of Lamb, 156
    Grilled Lamb Chops, *154*, 155
lasagna
    Philly Cheesesteak Lasagna, 147–148, *149*
    Seafood Lasagna, 128–129
lemonade
    Easy Strawberry Lemonade, 224, *225*
    Pink Moscato Lemonade, *226*, 227
lobster
    Loaded Baked Oysters, 66
    Mardi Gras Pasta Salad, 111
    Seafood Boil with Creole Garlic Sauce, *130*,
        131–132
    Seafood Lasagna, 128–129

M

Macaroni and Cheese Casserole, Southern
    Baked, 182–183
Macaroni Salad, Cousin Rosie's, 110
main dishes, 123–161
measuring cups, liquid vs. dry, 25
Meat Lover's Quiche, 42, *43*
Meat Pies with Creole Chimichurri, Southern,
    82–83, *83*

Mojito, Cherry, 233
Monkey Bread, Savory, *90*, 91
Muffuletta, *116*, 117

N

Neck Bones and Potatoes, Slow Cooker, *160*,
    161

O

Olive Salad, *116*, 117
Onions, Cajun Blooming, *58*, 59–60
Orzo Rice Pilaf, 180, *181*
Oxtails, Jamaican, 152, *153*
oysters
    Loaded Baked Oysters, 66
    Spicy Catfish and Oyster Po'boys, 118–119

P

pantry and fridge essentials, 9–21
Parsnips with Bacon, Roasted, 172
pasta
    Cajun Chicken Pasta Salad, *112*, 113
    Cousin Rosie's Macaroni Salad, 110
    Mardi Gras Pasta Salad, 111
    Orzo Rice Pilaf, 180, *181*
    Philly Cheesesteak Lasagna, 147–148, *149*
    Seafood Lasagna, 128–129
    Southern Baked Macaroni and Cheese
        Casserole, 182–183
Peach Cobbler Bread Pudding, *196*, 197
Peach Sweet Tea, Grown Folks, 230, *231*
Philly Cheesesteak Lasagna, 147–148, *149*
pies
    Blackberry Pie, 199–200, *201*
    Chocolate Chess Pie, *202*, 203
    Southern Meat Pies with Creole
        Chimichurri, 82–83, *83*
Pigeon Peas and Rice, 177
Pineapple Hennyrita, 228
Po'boys, Spicy Catfish and Oyster, 118–119

pork

See also bacon; sausage

Blackberry-Glazed Ribs, 158–159, *159*

Boudin Balls, 80–81

Cheddar, Ham, and Grits Casserole, *50*, 51

Cracklin' Cornbread, 88–89, *89*

Meat Lover's Quiche, 42, *43*

Muffuletta, *116*, 117

Slow Cooker Neck Bones and Potatoes, *160*, 161

Southern Meat Pies with Creole Chimichurri, 82–83, *83*

Stuffed Pork Chops, 157

Ultimate Breakfast Sandwich, 35

potatoes

Creamy Mashed Baby Reds, 170, *171*

Creole Loaded Potato Skins, 61–62, *63*

Egg, Sausage, and Potato Scramble, 36, *37*

Five-Cheese Hash Brown Casserole, 47

Slow Cooker Neck Bones and Potatoes, *160*, 161

Soulful Breakfast Enchiladas, *38*, 39–40

Stuffed Hash Browns, 48, *49*

poultry

Bacon-Wrapped Stuffed Chicken Thighs, 134, *135*

Best Damn Chicken and Dumplings, 136–137, *137*

Boudin Balls, 80–81

Butterflied Herb-Roasted Chicken, 133

Cajun Chicken Pasta Salad, *112*, 113

cleaning, tips for, 140

Collard Green and Smoked Turkey Dressing, 168–169

Deep-Fried Cornish Game Hens, *144*, 145–146

Easy Smoked Whole Turkey, *138*, 139–140

Fried Chicken Gizzards, 76–77, *77*

Fried Chicken Sliders, *78*, 79

Royal Wings, 75

Slow Cooker Smothered Turkey Wings, 141–142, *143*

Southern Meat Pies with Creole Chimichurri, 82–83, *83*

Waffle Fried Chicken, *44*, 45–46

Q

Quiche, Meat Lover's, 42, *43*

R

Red Velvet Biscuits, 95

Red Velvet Waffles, 30, *31*

ribs

Blackberry-Glazed Ribs, 158–159, *159*

Easy Slow Cooker Short Ribs, *150*, 151

rice

Boudin Balls, 80–81

Orzo Rice Pilaf, 180, *181*

Pigeon Peas and Rice, 177

White Beans and Sausage, *178*, 179

S

salads

Cajun Chicken Pasta Salad, *112*, 113

Cousin Rosie's Macaroni Salad, 110

greens, preparation tips for, 21

Mardi Gras Pasta Salad, 111

Not Yo' Mama's Bacon Caesar Salad, 108, *109*

Olive Salad, *116*, 117

salmon. *See* fish

sandwiches

Fried Chicken Sliders, *78*, 79

Fried Tilapia Sandwiches, 114, *115*

Muffuletta, *116*, 117

Spicy Catfish and Oyster Po'boys, 118–119

Ultimate Breakfast Sandwich, 35

sauces

Blackberry Glaze, 158–159

Cocktail Sauce, 67–68, *69*

Creole Chimichurri, 82, *83*

Creole Garlic Sauce, *130*, 131–132

Seasoned Butter, 139

Spicy Tartar Sauce, 118

Sweet Chili Sauce, 72, *73*

sausage

    Creole Loaded Potato Skins, 61–62, *63*

    Egg, Sausage, and Potato Scramble, 36, *37*

    Meat Lover's Quiche, 42, *43*

    Muffuletta, *116*, 117

    Savory Monkey Bread, *90*, 91

    Seafood Boil with Creole Garlic Sauce, *130*, 131–132

    Soulful Breakfast Enchiladas, *38*, 39–40

    Southern Meat Pies with Creole Chimichurri, 82–83, *83*

    Stuffed Hash Browns, 48, *49*

    White Beans and Sausage, *178*, 179

savory essentials, 17–21

Scones, Butter Pecan, *98*, 99

seafood

    See also fish

    Creole Crab Cakes with Sweet Chili Sauce, 72, *73*

    Grilled Creole Shrimp Cocktails, 67–68, *69*

    Jamaican Jerk Shrimp and Peppers, 124, *125*

    Loaded Baked Oysters, 66

    Mardi Gras Pasta Salad, 111

    Poached Garlic Crab Legs, 74

    Seafood Boil with Creole Garlic Sauce, *130*, 131–132

    Seafood Lasagna, 128–129

    Spicy Catfish and Oyster Po'boys, 118–119

    Voodoo Dip, 56, *57*

seasoning, over- vs. under-, 11

seasonings, essential, 10–14, *12*

7UP Cake, Moist, 215–216, *217*

Short Ribs, Easy Slow Cooker, *150*, 151

shrimp

    Grilled Creole Shrimp Cocktails, 67–68, *69*

    Jamaican Jerk Shrimp and Peppers, 124, *125*

    Seafood Boil with Creole Garlic Sauce, *130*, 131–132

    Seafood Lasagna, 128–129

    Voodoo Dip, 56, *57*

side dishes, 163–183

Simple Syrup, 224, 227

Sliders, Fried Chicken, *78*, 79

Slow Cooker Neck Bones and Potatoes, *160*, 161

Slow Cooker Short Ribs, Easy, *150*, 151

Slow Cooker Smothered Turkey Wings, 141–142, *143*

Smoked Whole Turkey, Easy, *138*, 139–140

Smothered Turkey Wings, Slow Cooker, 141–142, *143*

spices and herbs, 10–14, *12*

spinach. *See* greens

starters, 53–83

Strawberry Lemonade, Easy, 224, *225*

Strawberry Shortcake Cheesecake, *206*, 207–209

T

Tartar Sauce, Spicy, 118

tea, sweet

    Frozen Green Sweet Tea, 229

    Grown Folks Peach Sweet Tea, 230, *231*

Tea Cakes, Southern, 186–187

Tilapia Sandwiches, Fried, 114, *115*

tools, kitchen, 23–27

turkey. *See* poultry

Turnip Greens and Artichoke Au Gratin Dip, *54*, 55

V

Voodoo Dip, 56, *57*

W

Waffle Fried Chicken, *44*, 45–46

Waffles, Red Velvet, 30, *31*

Wings, Royal, 75

Wings, Slow Cooker Smothered Turkey, 141–142, *143*

CONVERSIONS

VOLUME

UNITED STATES	METRIC	IMPERIAL
¼ tsp.	1.25 ml	
½ tsp.	2.5 ml	
1 tsp.	5 ml	
½ Tbsp.	7.5 ml	
1 Tbsp.	15 ml	
⅛ c.	30 ml	1 fl. oz.
¼ c.	60 ml	2 fl. oz.
⅓ c.	80 ml	2.5 fl. oz.
½ c.	125 ml	4 fl. oz.
1 c.	250 ml	8 fl. oz.
2 c. (1 pt.)	500 ml	16 fl. oz.
1 qt.	1 l	32 fl. oz.

LENGTH

UNITED STATES	METRIC
⅛ in.	3 mm
¼ in.	6 mm
½ in.	1.25 cm
1 in.	2.5 cm
1 ft.	30 cm

WEIGHT

AVOIRDUPOIS	METRIC
¼ oz.	7 g
½ oz.	15 g
1 oz.	30 g
2 oz.	60 g
3 oz.	90 g
4 oz.	115 g
5 oz.	150 g
6 oz.	175 g
7 oz.	200 g
8 oz. (½ lb.)	225 g
9 oz.	250 g
10 oz.	300 g
11 oz.	325 g
12 oz.	350 g
13 oz.	375 g
14 oz.	400 g
15 oz.	425 g
16 oz. (1 lb.)	450 g
1½ lb.	750 g
2 lb.	900 g
2¼ lb.	1 kg
3 lb.	1.4 kg
4 lb.	1.8 kg

TEMPERATURE

OVEN MARK	FAHRENHEIT	CELSIUS	GAS
Very cool	250–275	130–140	½–1
Cool	300	150	2
Warm	325	165	3
Moderate	350	175	4
Moderately hot	375	190	5
	400	200	6
Hot	425	220	7
	450	230	8
Very Hot	475	245	9

Printed in China

SASQUATCH BOOKS with colophon is a registered trademark of Penguin Random House LLC

26 25 24 23 22   9 8 7 6 5 4 3 2 1

Editor: Susan Roxborough, Jen Worick
Production editor: Rachelle Longé McGhee
Designer: Tony Ong
Photographs: Michael Kartes
Food and prop styling: Danielle Kartes

Library of Congress Cataloging-in-Publication Data
Names: Mayes, Rosie (Food writer), author. | Kartes, Danielle,
   photographer. | Kartes, Michael, photographer.
Title: Super soul food with cousin Rosie : 100+ modern twists on comfort
   food classics / Rosie Mayes ; photography and styling by Michael and
   Danielle Kartes.
Description: Seattle : Sasquatch Books, [2022] | Includes index.
Identifiers: LCCN 2021060603 (print) | LCCN 2021060604 (ebook) | ISBN
   9781632174239 (paperback) | ISBN 9781632174246 (epub)
Subjects: LCSH: Cooking, American–Southern style. | Comfort food–
   Southern States. | LCGFT: Cookbooks.
Classification: LCC TX715.2.S68 M327 2022 (print) | LCC TX715.2.S68
   (ebook) | DDC 641.5975–dc23/eng/20211231
LC record available at https://lccn.loc.gov/2021060603
LC ebook record available at https://lccn.loc.gov/2021060604

The recipes contained in this book have been created for the ingredients and techniques indicated. Neither publisher nor author is responsible for your specific health or allergy needs that may require supervision. Nor are publisher and author responsible for any adverse reactions you may have to the recipes contained in the book, whether you follow them as written or modify them to suit your personal dietary needs or tastes.

ISBN: 978-1-63217-423-9

Sasquatch Books
1325 Fourth Avenue, Suite 1025
Seattle, WA 98101

SasquatchBooks.com

MIX
Paper from responsible sources
FSC® C001701
www.fsc.org